Notes on the State of America

A Compilation of Less Commonly Discussed Facts and Historical Events

By
Craighton E. Gee

Inspirasian® Press LLC
San Francisco, California

Gee, Craighton E.
    Notes on the State of America: A Compilation of Less Commonly Discussed Facts and Historical Events / Craighton E. Gee
    Includes bibliographical references and index
    ISBN 0-9743882-0-3
    1.   United States – Political Science - History - Foreign Relations – Philosophy

Printed in the United States   First printing – September, 2003
    Library of Congress Control Number: 2003110520

This book is dedicated to the common peoples in the world, unknown and uncelebrated, who in their own way gave their measure of contribution to the sincere establishment of real human rights, civil rights, democracy, liberty, and freedom.

ORDERING INFORMATION

To order additional copies of *Notes on the State of America*, a convenient form is included on the following page for either mail or fax.

Inspirasian Press can also send copies of the book directly to other people or organizations on your behalf. Simply complete the "Send to" section, and indicate whether or not you would like a short note enclosed with the book indicating that the gift is from you.

Inspirasian Press strives to make this book as widely available as possible. We operate under the belief that the widest possible distribution of the information contained in this book will be of great benefit to all people. If you would like to support this effort, Inspirasian Press also gladly accepts donations to apply to this work.

If you have corrections or comments (for future editions of this book), the author can be reached by sending your correspondence through Inspirasian Press at the mailing address below.

Please mail or fax orders to:

Inspirasian Press LLC
P. O. Box 460256
San Francisco, CA 94146-0256 (USA)

(Tel) 415-282-7925
(Fax) 415-282-6427
www.inspirasian.com

Yes, I would like to order copies of *Notes on the State of America*. Please send _____ copies at $10.00 each, plus $2.50 per book shipping ($3.50 for 2-4 books, $4.50 for 5-9 books). California residents please add $0.85 sales tax per book. Call or fax for shipping costs on larger or foreign orders.

Name _____
Company _____
Address _____
City, State, Zip _____
Telephone _____

Send to:
Name _____
Company _____
Address _____
City, State, Zip _____

_____ **Yes**, please enclose a note indicating that I sent this book as a gift.
_____ **No**, I wish this gift to remain anonymous. Please do not enclose a note.

_____ My check / money order is enclosed.
(Make check payable to Inspirasian Press LLC)
_____ Bill my _____ Visa _____ Mastercard
_____ American Express

Card Number _____
Expiration Date _____

Signature _____

TABLE OF CONTENTS

Notes on the State of America

Is This Book for You?

Do you feel that you, or someone that you know, would benefit from a fuller understanding of America's true history and from learning critical facts relevant to today's global problems and challenges? Would you like to understand the perspectives of people living outside of America, and do you want to base your conclusions on facts?

Do you believe in preserving America's founding principles? Do you support human and civil rights for *all* humans who inhabit our planet? Do you desire a safe and sustainable future for your children and humanity as a whole? Are you willing to learn information that may be contrary to what you may have been taught, and perhaps come from a far different perspective than you currently subscribe?

This book will give you a brief overview of America from a perspective different from the one you were likely exposed to in your formal education. You may find some of the material in this book quite familiar. On the other hand, you will likely find some of the information at the very least disturbing, or even startling or shocking. Every country's history is comprised of both historical events and facts that are both a source of pride and a source of shame. America is no different. Nevertheless, it is suggested that it is important for people to develop a realistic worldview so that they are in position to make well-informed judgments regarding important issues of the day.

This book presents less commonly discussed historical events and facts that may be construed as quite negative from America's perspective. This book was *intentionally* written in this manner so that the book might

1

serve as a supplement to add balance to many existing texts regarding American history that generally emphasize the country's many strengths and positive elements. The intention of this material is to encourage a more balanced perspective toward America and its place in the world.

The reader will also be exposed to quite a bit of information relating to international affairs. The content was intentionally written in the form of short overviews, in order to make the information easily digestible. Because America is a rich country with vast internal resources, its citizens have historically had the luxury to focus their attention primarily on domestic problems and domestic solutions. In today's global age, it is increasingly impossible to understand what is really happening within our own country, without some understanding of what is happening beyond our national borders.

America remains an unimaginable source of energy, creativity, and innovation primarily because of the diversity and energy of its people. America remains one of the freest societies in the world, and a top destination for people around the world who seek an opportunity to better their life condition. And with respect to most day-to-day activities, most American citizens can expect justice. But this is not the entire story of America, and it is important to have an accurate picture of our country if we are to play our part as American citizens.

If America is really a democracy - a governing system that is ruled by the people - then the people of America have a particular responsibility to use their power to steer their country in a direction that is truly reflective of the country's principles and values. People who live under a dictatorship do not have this type of responsibility, given that their governing system constricts their ability to act. Americans have this responsibility to act. This is the responsibility that comes with freedom and democracy.

For those of you who fear that by reading this book you will be considered by your community as unpatriotic or subversive, welcome to the company of many of America's noted citizens who dared to challenge prevailing thought during the times in which they lived.

About a decade after the American Revolution, Thomas Jefferson was considered a subversive outsider by political leaders close to President George Washington. Mr. Jefferson believed that the country was growing in an unhealthy direction; a direction that was not true to its founding principles. He decided to campaign as the 3rd president of our country and endured a horrific, brutal campaign to win back power that would allow him to implement new policy based on his views.

Simply put, Thomas Jefferson believed that the country was becoming what it had originally intended not to be; a European style aristocracy. To Jefferson, America was becoming no different in its class structure. He looked at America's governing elite, and likened them to the pampered and decadent royalty of Europe. He felt that a "fresh revolution" might be necessary. In fact, in its day, this chain of events was called the "second American revolution"; no less important than the first revolution.

When he was finally elected, President Jefferson threw open the doors of the White House to the public, arranged for the immediate release of political prisoners that were considered subversive by the previous administration, and even wrote letters of apology on behalf of the United States government.

If you fear being labeled unpatriotic, welcome also to the company of countless less known American citizens who played a part in American history, and the many better known people including:

The original "enlightenment thinkers" (e.g. Locke, Montesqueau, and Rousseau) who, prior to the American Revolution, wrote their ideas on paper and planted the seeds of fundamental democratic principles. It was their ideas that early colonists used to draft their own Declaration of Independence from Britain, and to create America's Constitution. These thinkers espoused revolutionary beliefs that, in aggregate, advanced the notion that common people are capable of self-governance; that the governance of man does not require a dictator or tyrant.

Abraham Lincoln, who preserved America as one country and in doing so, steered the country through one of its most difficult issues of the time – human slavery.

Frederick Douglass, who as a self-made free black man spent his lifetime working to gain the most basic rights of citizenship for African Americans. Many of his contemporaries simply could not believe that such an intellectual and articulate man could possibly be of slave origins.

Mark Twain, who through his writings held a critical mirror in front of Americans, and left us glad that we had looked. He wrote prolifically and with wit about his positions on many sensitive issues of his day. Among them race and American global imperialism.

Susan B. Anthony and Elizabeth Cady Stanton, women who fought a lifetime battle to secure citizenship and voting rights for women, and were not even alive to see the fruition of their goals.

Martin Luther King Jr., a servant and spokesperson for thousands of less-known people who really were collectively the real engine behind the civil rights movement.

All of these people challenged prevailing thought and custom. They tried, through personal action, to move the country toward a path truer to America's founding principles and ideals, however imperfect their efforts might be given the times that they lived and prevailing sentiment. They knew that America was (and still is) a young experiment – a "work-in-progress".

To give a long-term perspective, it is instructive to note that the earth is over 4.5 billion years old. Human history consists of only the most recent 200,000 years. Agricultural history began only about 20,000 years ago. Since that time, there have been many magnificent human civilizations that were really the origins of everything America enjoys today.

Pottery originated from Northern Africa, the Middle East, and Asia, the wheel from the Mesopotamia (current day Iraq) in the Middle East. Early agricultural practices originated in China, India, Egypt and Peru. Metal making developed in the Middle East, Europe, China, and the Andes.

Magnificent cities were constructed in Mesopotamia, Egypt, India, China (Shang, Zhou, and Han Dynasties), Mexico (Aztecs), South America (Incas), and in the Greek and Roman Empire.

Early writing came from Mesopotamia and Egypt, mathematics and measurement originated in Egypt, China, and from the Babylonians, Indians, Mayans, Greeks, and Romans.

Medicine has its roots in South America, China, Egypt, India, and the Greek and Rome civilizations.

Early engineering originated from Egypt, the Middle East, and the Aztec, Mayan, and Inca civilizations.

And within this long timeframe, America's lifetime is a mere 227-year heartbeat.

Americans like to believe that their country and their governing system have already proven themselves an unqualified success, largely because of our rapid economic growth and military strength. However, many civilizations throughout the world and throughout human history (both democratic and non-democratic, religious and non-religious) have endured far longer than America has thus far. The American democratic experiment is truly still in its early days, and has yet to prove itself as a long-term sustainable country and governing system.

The information in this book is certainly not comprehensive with regards to all possible American historical events and facts of interest. To create this particular compilation of information, the writer has relied heavily on decades of painstaking research that thousands of other people have done in order to publish their own credible sources of information. These sources are listed at the end of the book.

Although the book may be read from front to back, it is perhaps more useful to readers as a convenient reference book, a primer of sorts, covering a wide range of topics relating to America. It is also expected that new relevant information will be added to this book in the future. However, the reader will find that this book contains a compilation that will prove valuable with respect to developing a basic understanding of the various topics of interest.

Frankly, some people do not like to read or do not have much free time to read. This is understandable. For the convenience of the reader, at the beginning of each chapter there is a short summary for that chapter. It is suggested that the reader first read the short chapter summaries and skip the short sections within each chapter. Certain strong assertions will be made in those summaries, which will likely lead the reader to seek examples, data, or facts supporting these assertions. The reader can then get more detail by selectively reading any of the short topic sections within each chapter.

This book is designed for you to read at your convenience in small bites, and in random order (Who said that you must read a book from front to back?). Place this book in a convenient location, and randomly select and read a short paragraph whenever you have a free moment. Your purse, your briefcase, your book bag, on your nightstand, or by the latrine is perfect. You might want to share the information in this book with a friend. And when you are done reading the book, you might want to consider passing the book on to someone else that you think might benefit.

As previously mentioned, at the end of this book you will find a list of references for the information contained herein. Because of the nature of this book, information has been culled from a wide variety of sources. The reader is encouraged to independently pursue other sources of information to verify, or more clearly understand the events and facts discussed in this book.

Most people, however, don't have the interest or energy to gather and read large volumes of information. It is in this spirit that this book was created. The intent was to relieve this problem by providing brief summary discussions of American historical events, and by providing relevant facts and statistics regarding the country.

Notes on the State of America

A working American democracy also requires an informed and assertive citizenry, which is why the recent consolidation of the media industry (television, magazines, newspapers, movies, internet) is an important related topic. Each of us hold worldviews and values that are, in no small part, a reflection of the quality and diversity of the information that we receive, as well as the cultural tone that is set by our leaders in all spheres of endeavor. Many of the sections in this book will shed light on the troubling changes in American media.

Explore the information in this book, integrate it with what you already know, and draw your own conclusions based on your own personal values and morals. As you read the information contained in this book, ask yourself whether you think America has behaved (and not just talked) in a manner that sincerely supports human rights, civil rights, democracy, liberation, and freedom for all people on this planet. Consider whether American behavior has for too long been based too narrowly on self-interests, with an unsustainable disregard for the long-term health of our country and the broader world. Consider and then act.

The book ends with a personal perspective from the writer. The observations and suggestions for action are based on the information contained in this book, and the writer's worldview and value system. These thoughts are offered to advance the notion that if America is to remain a safe, prosperous, and sustainable civilization in the future, its citizens must have an accurate worldview and a capability to adjust America's direction as required.

Whatever you conclude, it is hoped that you will come away with a more well-informed and balanced perspective on which you can base your views on the important issues of our day.

On Human Rights, Civil Rights, Democracy, Liberty, and Freedom

Chapter Summary – America was founded in July of 1776 and first expressed itself through a remarkable document called the Declaration of Independence. The document was the result of a compilation and distillation of years of "enlightenment thinking" that postulated that human beings were born equal, that they were born with natural rights, that they had the capability to govern themselves without the rule of a king, and that the ultimate power of governance belong to the people. Early on, these founding concepts were extended and expressed deliberately and concisely in the American Constitution and Bill of Rights.

Because America originated with such a clearly expressed intent, the country immediately and irrevocably agreed to be held to a higher standard of conduct than other countries throughout the world that originated through primarily tribal or ancestral roots. Martin Luther King Jr., an American civil rights leader, termed this concept as "a promissory note" in his famous "I have a Dream" speech in Washington D.C. The promise being that all mankind is created equal, and that all mankind has a *natural* claim to life, liberty, and the pursuit of happiness. From this assertion evolved the concepts of Human Rights, Civil Rights, Democracy, Liberty, and Freedom.

Sadly and in reality, these concepts were not automatically and immediately granted to all mankind living in America. And also sadly, America's government has all too frequently acted in a manner in direct *contradiction* to these publicly expressed fundamental principles, both to people living within the country, and to those people living in other countries outside of America's national boundaries. This is a hypocrisy that, although understood to be a natural consequence of the imperfection of man, cannot stand over time simply because it flies in direct contradiction to why the country was founded in the first place.

In early years of colonial America, democracy, freedom, and liberty were extended exclusively to a narrow category of the American population, primarily white, wealthy, male landowners. Gradually over time, freedom and democratic rights were extended to other groups such as people of non-white descent, women, and labor classes.

This evolutionary change only occurred because of a long history of difficult struggle by activists, and through the prosecution of a long and costly American Civil War. It is only through these efforts, efforts that continue to the current day, that these five guiding principles were extended to all Americans. And, in virtually all cases, gains were accomplished primarily through the courage, sacrifices, and relentless effort of those groups that were disaffected. It was not accomplished through the benevolence of the American government or its elite upper classes. These social movements were powered by masses of people, and not individual leaders upon which American culture tends to focus.

Given the country's purported ideology, the American government has a surprising and recurrent history of destroying prospects for real democracy and freedom both at home and abroad. At home, this was to preserve a hierarchy and class system. Abroad, it was done primarily for three reasons: To halt the spread of "communist thought", to prevent independence from American control, or to pave the way for American big business interests.

Rights, Democracy, Liberty, and Freedom

It is strange and contrary to what most Americans believe that historically America's political and business leaders have aimed to suppress the development of prosperous, free and independent foreign nations. It was feared by these leaders that successful developing sovereign nations might become a model, which would encourage other people throughout the world to push for their own independence from American economic interests and geopolitical influence.

Capitalism is inextricably and intimately infused into American democracy. One cannot discuss American democracy without considering the concepts of American capitalism. Not surprisingly, this condition has often resulted in a corrosive effect on the democratic institution.

Governments use various types of tools to implement its policies, which are themselves an expression of political will. This political will can originate from the common people, but more often than not it is the political will of a wealthy elite. Governments use social and cultural contracts, whether explicitly documented or not. And they use a tool called "the law".

In contrast to how many people view the law, it has been observed throughout America's history of social upheaval and evolution that the law and the legal process serve primarily as a political tool designed to codify and execute political policy. Sometimes, and more likely on the less-important matters of the day, the law coincides with real justice. However, with regards to the larger and more important matters, the law has historically largely been used as a tool to implement political will of the wealthy classes often suppressing the rights of the common man.

America has an undeniably hypocritical and contradictory history regarding the concepts of Human

11

rights, Civil rights Democracy, Liberty, and Freedom, both at home and overseas. Numerous examples are set forth in the following section. American citizens will likely already be familiar with many of the examples from home, but may find some of the overseas examples interesting and perhaps even surprising.

The sections are short, each written to provide a very brief overview of each topic area. (There exist innumerable lengthy well-written books describing in detail many of the topics.) The writer has also intentionally made no attempt to justify or excuse the behavior or actions of the American government in any of the examples. The information in this section will establish a foundational context for understanding and connecting the information in the following sections of this book.

African American Slavery – From America's inception in the 1700's until the late 1800's, the trading and exploitation of people of primarily African descent was institutionalized into the country's political, legal, cultural, and economic system.

The early American colonists bought, sold, and held captive black slaves originating from Africa. Wealthy landowners used slaves as a source of free labor permitting the viability and rapid growth of profitable commerce, primarily for agricultural products such as cotton, tobacco, and sugar cane.

American slavery was supported through American law. An example is the 1857 Supreme Court Dred Scott decision, which ruled that slaves did not become free in a free state, that Congress could not bar slavery from a territory, and that blacks could not become citizens.

It is interesting to compare American slavery with, for example, Roman slavery. Roman slavery did not make a racial distinction, as members of all races could be considered a slave. Roman slavery was considered more of a social class, than an institution related to race. In contrast, American slavery aligned closely with race because of a pervasive fundamental white supremacy belief.

One theory for this race-based American slavery phenomenon is that as the institution of slavery became increasingly viewed as immoral, slaveholders needed a reason to morally justify their heinous behavior. By dehumanizing specific categories of people based on race, slaveholders allowed themselves a logical way in which they could feel justified for the immoral actions that they perpetrated on their slaves.

In 1859, a man by the name of John Brown attempted to start an armed revolution in America to halt the immoral practice of slavery. He seized an American federal arsenal at Harpers Ferry, Virginia. Most of his 21 compatriots (fugitive slaves, college students, free blacks, a neighbor, and three of his sons) died at Harpers Ferry, and John Brown was eventually hanged. But, before he died he was able to speak to journalists and spread impassioned messages advocating the total abolition of slavery. John Brown, through his unshakable devotion to the destruction of the institution of slavery, inspired further thousands of other committed abolitionists and spurred the country into the inevitable national Civil War conflict.

Even decades after the abolition of slavery in America, remnants of the early racist belief system and conditioning are still present in the American psyche and are slow to diminish as its citizens learn new thinking patterns. The anti-slavery movement and the subsequent civil rights movement were necessary steps toward a morally sustainable American culture. An estimated 20 million Africans were enslaved in America.

Jim Crow Era – The defeat of the Southern states in America's Civil War in the 1860s and Abraham Lincoln's Emancipation Proclamation did not halt the discrimination and oppression of African Americans. Many states and local jurisdictions immediately adopted a series of "Jim Crow" laws that were clearly designed to continue African American subjugation. These laws were supported and validated by the United States Supreme Court "separate but equal" segregation ruling.

It is not well known by most Americans that Abraham Lincoln's Emancipation Proclamation applied only to the Southern states in rebellion, and did not apply to the other states that remained in the Union. Lincoln's proclamation was calculatingly crafted to encourage the sizeable black population in the South to rise up against the Southern armies and civilian population, which would in turn help the North win the war and preserve the union.

While personally abhorring the institution of slavery, Abraham Lincoln's earliest objective was always to preserve the union of the United States of America, and not to free the slaves. Lincoln stated, "My paramount object in this struggle (civil war) is to save the union, and not either to save or to destroy slavery. If I could save the union without freeing any slave, I would do it. And, if I could save it by freeing all the slaves, I would do it. And, if I could save it by freeing some and leaving others alone, I would also do that." However, despite these early motivations, by the end of the Civil War President Lincoln had come to hold a genuine deep commitment to the total abolition of slavery throughout America.

Ku Klux Klan and Neo Nazism – In 1866, shortly after the Southern states surrendered the Civil War, an organization named the Ku Klux Klan was secretly formed in the South and was intended to terrorize blacks attempting to vote. After a few years in operation, the organization disbanded but was resurrected and reorganized in 1915. This ushered in decades of brutal and violent repression of blacks, primarily in the South.

Remnants of the white supremacist and anti-Semitic thought adopted by groups such as the Ku Klux Klan, the White Citizens Council, the Nazi Party, and other racist organizations remain in contemporary Neo Nazi ideology. The hate philosophies of this group have expanded to include all non-whites, homosexuals, and whites that do not share the same beliefs as them.

Labor Movement – After decades of worker exploitation and as a part of a global movement during the early 1900s, American workers began to organize into trade unions and fight for shorter hours, higher wages, and better working conditions.

In fact, the early part of the century was rife with violent labor disputes throughout the world. American business, many times with a complaisant government, attempted to suppress the budding labor movement. American business leaders were staunchly opposed to relinquishing any measure of control over the workplace and losing any power to decide on the allocation business profits. They were often willing use open deceit and even violence to oppose such changes in American business practices.

Workers from a wide range of industries began massive strikes for better conditions. These industries included the garment (over 40,000 laborers participated in initial labor strikes), steel, coal, and food processing industries.

In order to intimidate labor leaders and their supporters, powerful business and political leaders not often accused them (rightly or wrongly) of being Communists. In fact, any movement that advocated a broader distribution of wealth was extremely threatening to the elite wealthy capitalists in early America.

As an example of their strong reaction to the budding labor movement, during the early 1900s public relations budgets for big business increased by a factor of 20 in order to combat what was seen as a dangerous growth of "power by the masses".

Woman's Suffrage Movement – For much of early world history, women were considered the property of and expected to be subservient to men. Despite the fact that Abigail Adams, wife of 2nd American President John Adams, urged early American colonists to include women in the Declaration of Independence (which the men refused), for the first 153 years of American history, women were denied even the most basic rights of citizenship.

Women had no voting rights, they had no property rights, any property owned by women immediately became the man's property upon marriage, women could not make a will, and women did not have power over decisions regarding their children upon a husband's death. These are only a few of the rights denied to women.

Ironically, many countries throughout the world had already for years granted women the vote. America, ostensibly a global leader for democracy, was a follower in this world trend.

The struggle to secure the rights of American citizenship for women began in earnest in the early 1800s, but it was not until 1929 that women finally won their right to the vote. This struggle required relentless sacrifice and work by thousands of Americans.

It is interesting to note that there was a definite hierarchy in the progression of voting rights in America: White men, Non-white men, White women, Non-white women. As a matter of fact, in their own struggle to win the vote, white women were forced to defer first to the granting of voting rights to the black man (although in reality, black men often still did not exercise their legal right to vote because they were impeded and even threatened with violence by local citizens). This hierarchy in the progression of voting rights was a significant point of contention between abolitionists such as Frederick Douglass and women's activists such as Susan B. Anthony and Elizabeth Cady Stanton.

Therefore, equality and fairness did not come either quickly or uniformly in American history. And, contrary to romanticized versions of American history, equality and fairness was virtually never granted through the benevolence or sense of fairness from the government. They were won through sustained and painstaking efforts of committed activists, growing political pressure, and at times violent action.

Chinese Exclusion Act and Anti-Chinese Laws – American immigrants of Chinese ancestry became the first group in the United States to face national immigration legislation designed specifically to block immigration to America based solely on race.

In 1882, America adopted a law, the Chinese Exclusion Act, which denied immigrants of Chinese ancestry admittance to the United States. With the exception of teachers, students, merchants, diplomats, and tourists, all other persons of Chinese ancestry were banned from immigrating to America. They could also not become citizens of America.

This draconian exclusion act was the culmination of a viciously racist and brutal movement within the United States that viewed American immigrants of Chinese ancestry as subhuman aliens and a dangerous competitive threat to poor white laborers. This law remained in place for 61 years, finally being repealed in 1943 primarily because the American government needed China to become an ally during World War II.

This exclusion action was invoked despite the fact that during the 1800s, it was the Chinese immigrants who were responsible for much of the life-threatening construction of the critical transcontinental railroad, fueling the country's subsequent economic and geographic expansion for decades to come. The work was extremely dangerous, and many literally gave their lives to complete this project.

Chinese immigrants were also part of the group of immigrants, primarily from Asia, who were responsible for the massive reclamation and cultivation of thousands of acres of land for agriculture. In fact, American immigrants from China accounted for fully 9 out of 10 farmers in early California. Because of their early efforts, and the efforts of their agricultural predecessors, California eventually became an undisputedly powerful productive agricultural region (with the attendant economic benefits) in America and even throughout the world.

During the second half of the 1800's and well into the 1900's, persons of Chinese ancestry were subjected to a succession of national, state, and local laws, ordinances, and regulation specifically crafted to discriminate and subjugate the Chinese population. These laws denied Chinese immigrants a wide range of basic rights, including those involving property rights and the right to testify against a white person in a court of law.

It is not well known by most Americans that the Chinese community in America repeatedly challenged virtually all of the racist laws that were enacted. In fact, it was in large part due to the legal challenges by the Chinese community that led to the securing of the important birth right citizenship. The right of citizenship upon birth subsequently benefited the children of all new immigrants, and distinguished America from many other nations in preventing the formation of a permanent underclass based on race.

Internment of Japanese, Italians, and Germans – In clear violation of the purported American ideals of fairness, democracy, freedom, liberty, and civil rights, the American government enacted laws that imprisoned persons of Japanese, Italian, and German ancestry living in America during World War II. The American History Dictionary defines concentration camps as "a camp where prisoners of war, enemy aliens, and political prisoners are confined". This was an American concentration camp.

Shortly after the surprise bombing of Pearl Harbor on Dec 7, 1941, President Franklin D. Roosevelt issued Executive Order 9066 mandating the evacuation, relocation, and internment of 120,000 people of Japanese ancestry living on the West Coast, 2/3 of them American citizens. These Japanese prisoners remained confined in camps throughout the duration of the war. They were given virtually no time to liquidate their property and

19

possessions before being imprisoned. Thus, it was not uncommon for Japanese internees to lose all their accumulated wealth. 11,000 persons of German ancestry and upwards of 250 persons of Italian ancestry also served time in American internment.

This was yet another dark episode in American history, one blatantly in contradiction to its purported national values. In fact, after decades, the American government was eventually forced to acknowledge the crime and issued an apology and granted some token reparations.

Ironically, at the same time that the United States government imprisoned citizens of Japanese descent, an American military regiment comprised of Japanese American soldiers managed to become the most highly decorated military regiment during World War II. They were known to be fearless and immensely courageous in fighting on behalf of America.

What is less known to most Americans is the fact that the American government initiated and orchestrated the forced deportation of 2,264 men, women, and children of Japanese ancestry living in 13 Latin American countries (of whom 80% were Japanese Peruvians). Put another way, the American government reached outside of its national borders to imprison innocent people, many of who were already legal citizens of other countries.

Passports were confiscated from these prisoners prior to their entry into the United States, and thus could be classified by the American government as "illegal aliens". They could therefore be incarcerated in Department of Justice internment camps. The American government kidnapped, arrested and held these people for the purpose of being used in future hostage exchanges with the enemy. Many were used in hostage exchanges.

The American government also treated 4,058 German and 288 Italian residents of Latin American countries in a like manner.

Japan – In the early years following World War II, the United States government did a surprising "about face" with regards to democracy in occupied Japan. General Douglas MacArthur was sent by the United States government to Japan to oversee the country's reconstruction after the end of World War II. MacArthur's administration took initial early steps ostensibly to guide Japan toward democratization.

However, in 1947 the American government changed its policy toward Japan and initiated a "reverse course" action. This new policy was crafted to deliberately suppress worker unions and other growing democratic activity, and place control of Japan firmly into the hands of corporate entities that backed Japanese facism. The legacy of this structure is what has become the Japanese political and economic system in the decades to follow. The immensely powerful Keiretsus (interlocking Japanese corporations) became the foundation of Japanese political and economic structure.

Control of Japan's government was eventually transferred back to the Japanese people, but only after the American government ensured that the country was developing in alignment with its own terms, and was largely controlled by American interests.

Civil Rights Movement – One year after a 1954 Supreme Court decision ruled that racial segregation in public schools was in violation of the American Constitution, a black activist by the name of Rosa Parks traveling on a public bus refused to give up her seat to a white man. This simple act, as often does, ignited a decades-long struggle for civil rights that had been percolating for years.

The resulting 80-day bus boycott in Montgomery, Alabama to protest segregation on public buses was led in part by a prominent black minister and civil rights leader, Martin Luther King Jr. This seminal protest action eventually led to the broad outlawing of segregation in all forms of public transportation, by the United States Supreme Court. It also inaugurated in a tumultuous and turbulent time in American history.

During the 1950s and 1960s, thousands of protestors participated in "freedom bus rides" from Northern cities to the South to protest racial discrimination in American laws. Many protestors were turned back or violently beaten by local authorities and thugs, and many of the protestor buses were set on fire.

By 1960, 50,000 people had demonstrated in over 100 American cities, and resulted in over 3,600 jailed protestors. The widespread brutality perpetrated against demonstrators by local law enforcement personnel became visible to the American people through the new medium of television broadcasting.

As one example of the level of brutality, police raided the house of Fred Hampton, a 21-year old charismatic African-American activist leader, and another fellow activist. Mr. Hampton had been previously demonized in the media and was considered a dangerous revolutionary. He was assassinated in a shower of bullets while in his bed. It is largely understood that by that point in time, the FBI had already concluded internally that the Black Panther Party (the activist group of which Mr. Hampton was a leader) needed to be destroyed.

It is of interest to note that during the turbulent years of the anti-Vietnam War and civil rights movement, activist veterans attest to the fact that there was a type of "white privilege". This term described the phenomenon that in American culture and among law enforcement personnel, it was acceptable for a black activist to be assassinated, but it was unacceptable for a white activist to be assassinated. White activists could be harassed and even beaten, but rarely or never assassinated.

Opposition to civil rights for blacks was particularly vehement among the politicians, legal bodies, police, and citizens in the Southern states, although resistance (and certainly not discrimination) was not isolated to the South. Young people who were active in bringing the black vote to Southern states were often beaten or even murdered.

During the Civil Rights movement, Martin Luther King Jr., quoted President John Kennedy in one of his speeches stating, "those that make peaceful protest impossible, make violent protest inevitable". It was in this volatile environment that organizations were established that actively worked on civil rights issues.

Some of these organizations were the Southern Christian Leadership Conference (SCLC that included as members, Martin Luther King Jr., Jessie Jackson, and Ralph Abernathy), Students Nonviolent Coordinating Committee (SNCC), National Association for the Advancement of Colored People (NAACP), Black Panthers and the Nation of Islam.

During these turbulent years, FBI Chief Herbert Hoover initiated widespread (legal and illegal) spying and harassment of civil rights leaders in an attempt to control civil rights activist activity. He frequently justified his secretive activity, at least what was publicly known, in the name of national security.

America's civil rights struggle culminated in a 200,000 person march for civil rights in Washington DC, and the passing of a new Voting Rights Act. United States Attorney General Robert Kennedy actively counseled his brother, President John Kennedy, to be more vocal in his support for civil rights, which he did.

In addition to many lesser-known civil rights participants, celebrated leaders including John Kennedy, Malcolm X, Martin Luther King Jr. and Robert Kennedy were assassinated. When Martin Luther King Jr. was assassinated, riots broke out in 167 cities resulting in 46 deaths, 21,000 injuries, 23,000 arrests, and scores of burned buildings.

It should be noted that the liberal "hippies" of that turbulent time period were actually one of the first groups in America to begin to embrace a new philosophy of genuine racial equality and common humanity. It was also during the 1960s that African American, Asian American and Latin American students and teachers demanded the establishment of ethnic studies programs to preserve and make accessible alternative sources of information and history.

Joseph McCarthy House Un-American Hearings – During the 1950s, fueled by intense fear within the American government (and hence the public), a Republican senator from Wisconsin by the name of Joseph McCarthy embarked on a crusade to uncover potential or actual communists living in America. His hearings were often conducted in clear violation of American due process and constitutional rights.

Within this climate of national fear, the anti-communism crusade was used also as a tool of harassment and repression by white supremacists against black civil rights leaders, by employers against emerging unions, and by sexual moralists against homosexuality.

Many lives and careers were destroyed. The United States Senate eventually censored the Senator. In the end, not one witness served time for being a dommunist, primarily because the accusations were unfounded and cases were discredited.

Third World Nationalism – During the 19th and 20th centuries, the United States government had a recurrent history of installing and supporting foreign leaders throughout the world that blatantly violate human rights, civil rights, democracy, liberty, and freedom. The government engaged in these activities to secure control over foreign activities, and to ensure foreign countries governed and acted in a manner supporting America's commercial and geopolitical interests.

In fact, high level United States administration documents have openly stated that the primary threat to a new American-led world order was something called "third world nationalism"; sometimes called "ultra-nationalism" or "nationalistic regimes". In general, these terms described governments that were authentically responsive to improving the poor living conditions affecting the masses of people in their countries. They were also governments that advocated governing systems that allocated the wealth of domestic production to serve the interests of the masses of people, rather than only the elite wealthy few.

These types of foreign governments have always been perceived as a threat by American government and

American corporate interests, because these alternative systems of government challenged the strongly entrenched ideologies of capitalism. These foreign governing systems were therefore considered un-American.

Budding popular revolutions in countries such as Cuba, El Salvador, Nicaragua, and Chile were serious threats to large American corporations such as United Fruit, Anaconda Copper, and ITT. Therefore military operations in foreign countries, whether conducted by American-trained foreign troops or American troops themselves, were presented to the American public as occurring for "national security interests", when they were really happening for corporate special interests.

In general, the American government likes countries to be run by regimes that will allow for private investment of American capital, will engage in trade, will keep their labor and other business costs down, and will allow profits to be taken out of the foreign country and repatriated (brought back) to the United States. The American government has not been as much concerned with the type of foreign regime (dictatorship, democratic, socialist, even brutal tyranny), so long as the regime serves America's strongly capitalistic interests.

Countries where parliamentary governments have been barred or overthrown through American action include Iran in 1953, the Dominican Republic in 1963 and 1965, Brazil in 1964, and Chile in 1973. Many specific examples are discussed in this chapter, and the chapters on Genocide and International Aggression.

Iran – For years, the American government had supported and backed a corrupt dictator, the Shah of Iran. The Shah of Iran had a formidable security force, and a particularly terrifying intelligence service.

In 1953, after many attempts, a populist uprising by the Iranian people finally prevailed which resulted in exile for the Shah, and the establishment of a popular democratic government under Prime Minister Mussadegh. This new popular government moved to nationalize the oil industry, meaning that oil production and distribution in Iran would be owned and controlled by the government, rather than private companies.

The British government became nervous because they were concerned with their investments and access to Iranian oil. Oil investment and access to oil resources in Iran were the primary driving impetus for some type of action. At the same time, the American government was in a frenzied fear over the spread of communism, and it feared its lack of control over potentially pro-communist people in the new democratic Iranian government.

The United States CIA worked to overthrow the new budding democracy in Iran. A successful coup ended the Mussadegh government and the brief exile of the Shah. The American government reinstalled the exiled pro-western dictator and continued to support the rule of the Shah. After the coup, the American government negotiated for a share of Iranian oil. In the end, British companies received access to 60% of the oil, and the remaining available Iranian oil was split between American and European companies. For more information regarding the historical implications of access to petroleum resources, please refer to the Oil Interests section.

Despite the fact that the Shah reestablished power in Iran, another subsequent populist revolution in 1979 finally ousted the Shah permanently and replaced him with a new leader, the Ayatollah Khomeini. Since that time, American government relations with the Iranian government have been tense, and the Iranian people have not forgotten that America in 1953 denied them their own chance to have real democracy in their own country.

During the 1980s, Iran fought an 8-year war with Iraq in which the United States government supported Iraq's Saddam Hussein (for further details, please see Saddam Hussein's Weapons Supplier section) with military and intelligence resources. Iran eventually lost over 300,000 lives in the protracted war.

In 1982, Israel invaded Lebanon. (Details regarding the United States government's history and ongoing relationship with Israel is discussed in detail in the Israel section.)

Iran supported the growing resistance movement to the Israeli invasion, and this conflict eventually gave rise to the emergence of HizbAllah, which became considered by the American government as a dangerous terrorist organization. Eventually, Israel withdrew their military forces from Lebanon in 2000.

However, unknown to most Americans, since the Lebanese War many in the Middle Eastern world already considered themselves engaged in a war of resistance against invasion and oppression by both Israel and the United States. And, because of the extreme imbalance with regards to weapons and military capabilities, many Middle Eastern resistance fighters have had to rely on the only real alternative that they have: guerilla and terrorist tactics.

In 1997, a new leader came to power in Iran, Mohammad Khatami, who has been more favorably received by the United States government. Presently, the Iranian people are split between those that desire a democratic system of government, and those that desire a governing system reliant on a "supreme leader".

In sheer irony, the American government which acted to deny democracy for Iran for over 25 years is now presenting itself as the staunch advocate and potential deliverer of Iranian democracy. At the same time, the United States administration is leveling hostile rhetoric and actions toward the Iranian government similar in tone and intent to what was done toward Saddam Hussein in Iraq.

These actions include the vilification and demonization of the Iranian government, a well-orchestrated and ubiquitous media and public relations campaign to the American people and the world, the support and aid of Iranian government dissenters, and pressure on international agencies, such as the global nuclear energy watchdog International Atomic Energy Agency (IAEA) and the United Nations Security Council, to take strong action with respect to Iran.

In further irony, given America's actual history toward democracy in Iran, in a recent State of the Union address the American President singled out and labeled Iran as one of the three countries constituting a global "Axis of Evil".

Haiti – As far back as 1803, the United States government has opposed Haitian freedom and independence from France. There was an expressed fear at the time that Haiti might become another one of the few "Black Republics" in the world, which is meant to signify a nation ruled primarily by black people. The American government, in fact, intervened in Haiti for a second time in 1915, and even kept American troops there for over 19 years.

In 1991, the American government supported an upcoming openly democratic Haitian election because they expected that their favored candidate, a former World Bank official by the name of Marc Bazin, would easily win office. Shockingly, a person by the name of Jean-Bertrand Aristide surprised the world by unexpectedly winning the free and democratic election in Haiti.

Aristide was swept into office largely because of a widespread and largely discounted grassroots movement, which resulted in an unexpected flood of votes from poor Haitian people. When the results were finally tallied, it was not even close. Aristide received 67% of the vote and Bazin received only 14% of the vote.

Aristide took office, and during the first seven months of his administration, he apparently made amazing progress regarding improving the conditions of the Haitian country and its people. In fact, progress was so good that even wealthy global lending institutions viewed Haiti under the Aristide regime positively, which bode well for future investment and financing for Haiti's development.

The American government set out to undermine the freely elected Aristide regime. In a country that had for decades been ruled by dictatorships with no American objection, the United States government launched a campaign to oust the Aristide regime, ostensibly under the humanitarian guise of "promoting democracy".

A military coup occurred in September of 1991, which included the slaughter of civilians in Haiti's capital, Port-au-Prince. Ironically, the American government blocked the migration of refugees fleeing for their lives from Haiti, which is in direct violation of the Universal Declaration of Human Rights the United States ostensibly supports. There is documented evidence that many of the refugees who were turned back by the United States government were subsequently hacked to death on the streets in Haiti.

During this same time period, the American government was continuing to actively review and consider immigration applications from far less credible (or entirely non-credible as deemed by United States immigration officials) refugees purportedly fleeing violent political persecution in Cuba under Fidel Castro.

After the military coup, Marc Bazin was eventually installed as the Haitian Prime Minister. The democratic popular organizations that got Aristide elected in the first place were destroyed. Terror and atrocities increased. And, American factories continue to produce baseballs and softballs for the great American pastime, while their American corporate employers pay poor Haitian workers 5-10 cents per hour to make them.

Brazil – Prior to 1964, Brazilians experienced rapid and dramatic changes due to a popular democracy movement in that country. The American government, however, increasingly perceived the Brazilian government as too successful and perhaps too independent of American interests. Consequently, the American government enthusiastically supported a military coup in Brazil, and stood by as new military leaders instituted a neo-Nazi style national security structure including torture, murder, and repression.

Brazil happens to be a country rich in vast natural resources. Despite this fact, and as commonly happens in these situations, an elite ruling Brazilian government largely followed the international and fiscal policy edicts of American economic advisors which eventually decimated the local Brazilian economy.

The Brazilian government was forced to became even more reliant on international finance bodies such as the International Monetary Fund (IMF) and World Bank to borrow money. For more explanation regarding these bodies, see the International Monetary Fund and United Nations World Bank section.

The IMF and World Bank commonly require economic prescriptions for governments (affecting for example, the handling of foreign currency, interest rates, domestic spending, international trade, and privatization) before providing financial support. These economic prescriptions tend often result in an economy that is vulnerable to wealthy foreign business interests desiring to penetrate local markets, repatriate profits, and at times even control the country.

It is not uncommon that these prescribed government and economic "reforms" are presented to the American and global community though the media as being in the best interest of the developing country (a benevolent act of America). The result is often a grossly tiered society consisting of a tiny number of people in a super-rich class, served by a small but larger comfortable professional class, with the masses of people comprised of workers or unemployed in a huge poverty class. Some experts have even noted that today, the economic situation for many Brazilians are on par with Ethiopia, with a higher infant mortality rate than Sri Lanka.

Chile - The United States government has an extended history of disrupting free democratic elections in Chile. The United States government disrupted their elections in 1964, and again in 1970. The American government has even threatened and acted to destroy the economy of Chile to achieve its aims.

Salvador Allende was a democratically elected social-democrat president of Chile, much in the style of many European politicians. President Allende was a respected doctor who worked toward the broader redistribution of wealth that would help the poor. He provided food to malnourished children, and he called for the nationalization of natural resources such as copper so that the government could allocate its wealth to the Chilean people (rather than to concentrate the wealth into privately owned companies). He also favored independence from foreign rule, and hence independence from American political and economic pressure.

During this time period, American Secretary of State Henry Kissinger characterized Chile as a threat; as a "virus" that would infect the Latin American region. In other words, a successful Chile might inspire other nations to seek increased sovereignty and independence from America, and even possibly lead other countries to adopt governing systems different from what the American government wanted in Chile in order to protect its own national interests.

The American President at the time considered two ways to handle the Chile situation: A "soft line" which would invoke severe economic and trade measures to perpetrate the "utmost deprivation and poverty" on the poor Chilean people, or a "hard line" which would consist of an outright military coup against the legitimately elected Allende government. The latter option was set in motion.

The United States CIA planted stories in the press, and fomented labor unrest and strikes. The campaign to remove Allende from office was aided by a large

American corporation with business interests in Chile, International Telephone and Telegraph (ITT). In 1973, President Allende was assassinated in an American-backed military coup. In all, the American government provided military training and $8 million in finance to destabilize the Allende government.

After the military coup, thousands of people were imprisoned, tortured, and murdered. Once the new American-backed administration took power, America's economic policy toward Chile was reversed and financial aid and support was approved for Chile. Henry Kissinger said, "I don't see why we have to let a country go Marxist just because its people are irresponsible."

Since then, reports have noted that while the American government would characterize Chile as a democratic country, it actually behaves much more like a nation governed under military rule.

Gay and Lesbian Movement – Historically, the United States government and a large portion of its people have viciously discriminated and attacked this population of its citizens through policy, laws, and culture. And, in fact, many of the most active and vocal proponents of discriminatory policy against gays and lesbians in America have been fundamentalist religious organizations. In 1943, even the United States military issued regulations barring gay and lesbians from serving in the armed forces.

However, recent decades in American history have indicated progress for gay and lesbian civil rights activists. In 1961, Illinois was the first state to abolish its anti-homosexual laws. In 1963, a brilliant gay leader by the name of Bayard Rustin organized Martin Luther King's famous Civil Rights March on Washington.

And in 1969, the Stonewall Inn bar was the site of a famous gay and lesbian rebellion to continuing police harassment. This landmark event has been considered by many to be the seminal event of the modern day gay and lesbian liberation movement.

Tragically, during the early 1980s, sexual orientation discrimination was a key factor for the American government's delayed response to an immensely serious mysterious health threat that first appeared in the gay community. The government's response was very slow primarily because the disease appeared to impact only two groups historically discriminated against; homosexuals and drug users. Initial victims were also hemophiliacs and other users of blood products, but they were also a small minority.

It was only after decades of AIDS (Acquired Immune Deficiency Syndrome) devastation, intense and relentless activism by the gay and lesbian community and their supporters, and the eventual spread of the disease into the heterosexual community that the American government launched a significant response against the disease.

Discrimination due to sexual orientation is still alive in America. In 2003, the United States Justice Department refused to allow an annual gay and lesbian event celebrating gay pride month at the agency's headquarters. This is the federal agency tasked with protecting the civil rights of all Americans (for more information relating to this agency, see Movement toward a Police State section). This discriminatory action was taken despite the fact that many other groups have been allowed to hold events at the site.

The department ultimately reversed its decision, claiming that the action was the result of a simple misunderstanding.

Post-9/11 Foreign Nationals Roundup – After the attack on the World Trade Center in September 2001, United States federal and local law enforcement personnel rounded up 762 foreign nationals (both legal and illegal immigrants), primarily of Middle Eastern descent. For all practical purposes, these people virtually disappeared from public sight.

A report issued significantly later in June of 2003 by the United States Justice Department inspector general's office, finally disclosed that the round up was plagued with problems. The end result of the round up was that many people with absolutely no connection to the September 11 attack languished in jails for months under harsh conditions, including physical and verbal abuse.

In fact, some prisoners were picked up at random traffic stops, and others were picked up simply because of anonymous reports that they were Muslims with "erratic schedules". The most basic civil and immigrant rights were summarily denied the prisoners. It was concluded that in processing the prisoners, the FBI (particularly in New York City), did little to distinguish between immigrants with credible terrorist ties and those who were simply rounded up by chance during the investigation. The report also determined that senior officials at the Justice Department did not heed voiced concerns regarding the legality of their aggressive tactics, even by their own internal legal counsel.

Ultimately, none (zero) of the 762 suspects in the round up were charged as terrorists.

A second extensive review of the post-9/11 immigrant roundup (based on actual data, analysis, and interviews) was soundly critical of the Justice Department actions, and determined that their action did little or nothing to improve national security. The study noted that the American government's post-9/11 actions were part of a historical pattern that included the internment of Japanese Americans during World War II (for details, see the Internment of Japanese, Italians, and Germans section), the deportation of Eastern European immigrants during the Red Scare from 1919-1920, and the internment of German Americans during World War I.

Finally, another subsequent report issued by internal investigators at the Justice Department noted credible incidents of civil rights and civil liberties violations involving law enforcement activities set in motion by the security crackdown which was supported by the USA Patriot Act. The specified activities include beatings of Muslim and Arab immigrants in federal detention centers.

Zacarias Moussaoui is a well-publicized and only major potential suspect that may be prosecuted by the Justice Department for the September 11 attack. In June 2003, the Justice Department pressured an American federal appeals court panel to prevent Moussaoui's attorneys access to a potential witness at Guantanamo Bay, who's testimony might exonerate Moussaoui from involvement with the September 11 attack.

United States officials estimate that of the 82,000 Arab and Muslim immigrants that were caught in counter-terrorism sweeps, voluntarily appeared before immigration service offices, and screened at airports and border crossings over the past 6 months, only 11 suspects had any possible links to terrorism (approximately 0.0001%).

Guantanamo Bay and Iraq Prisons – Guantanamo Bay is an American military site located in Cuba (for details regarding how the United States retained a site in Cuba, see Cuba section). After the events of September 11, the American government arrested and detained a large number of people at Guantanamo Bay, an isolated location distant from potential scrutiny by the American people.

These prisoners, many captured in Afghanistan, are from 42 countries and various national backgrounds, primarily Middle Eastern. The United States government has categorized them not as prisoners-of-war, but as "enemy combatants" thus making their legal status and rights unclear. This was done despite the fact that most of the detainees at Guantanamo Bay were captured on battlefields and would normally be considered prisoners-of-war. This was also done in violation of international law regarding political prisoners.

This alternative categorization of the prisoners in Guantanamo Bay by the United States government has allowed American military forces wide latitude regarding the rights of the political prisoners. This includes many of the very same rights that the American government has historically demanded of other nations.

The political prisoners have been held without charges or even access to lawyers. As of May 2003, after the end of major combat in the Iraq War, there were 680 political prisoners, and another 1,800 "unreleased prisoners" in Iraq. By August 2003, the estimated number of people held in Iraq by the American government has mushroomed to over 3,000.

Amnesty International, a respected human rights organization, has documented and publicly voiced serious concerns regarding excessive force, inhumane conditions, and a complete lack of transparency and accountability by the American military forces managing the prisoners in Iraq. Reported conditions include forced prolonged sleep deprivation, restraint of prisoners in painful positions, loud music and bright lights, and the use of tight hoods over heads.

The American government has indicated that in the processing of political prisoners, only military personnel will be allowed to act as both the judge and jury in an American military tribunal. Defendants will not be allowed to speak to their legal representatives in private, and there will be no independent non-military review process. Many reputable lawyers within the United States have already declined to participate in such a trial, because of its blatant partiality.

Also of note is that as of May 2003, over 1 year after initial detainment, 18 political prisoners at Guantanamo Bay have attempted suicide (some prisoners have tried multiple times to kill themselves) for a total of 27 suicide attempts. Global and domestic human rights groups have harshly criticized the United States regarding its handling of its political prisoners both at Guantanamo Bay and in prison facilities in Iraq. These groups have also indicated that the interrogation techniques used at Guantanamo Bay may include torture (see related Afghanistan section).

United Nations (UN) and the Security Council – The United Nations was formed shortly after World War II because the world recognized a need for a formal international institution that could serve as a forum to address issues of global importance, often issues relating to global security, military action, and foreign aid.

The Security Council, arguably the most powerful entity within the UN, is the political arm that considers international resolutions (statements of position, often precursors to allocation of money or deployment of military personnel) pertaining to military action and peacekeeping forces.

The Security Council is often perceived as a highly democratic institution. However, there are only a very small number of countries that are permanent voting members of the 15-member Security Council, while the rest of the countries rotate into the Security Council on a temporary basis. The permanent voting members include only wealthy industrialized countries or other countries perceived as influential or powerful by some other measure.

The permanent voting members in the council are the United States, Russia, China, France, and Britain. Any substantial (non-procedural) resolution from the Security Council can be passed only if every one of the 5 permanent members agrees to the resolution. Therefore, any one of the 5 permanent members has a powerful veto vote that can stop the passing of any Security Council resolution of importance.

Since 1970 the United States has vetoed, by far, the most number of Security Council and General Assembly resolutions than any other country. This American veto was invoked either to protect self-interests or as favors to those countries that are friends. The British have the second highest number of vetoes, France is a distant third, and then the Soviet Union. Israel, Jordan, and Turkey have been in violation of the most United Nations resolutions. Iraq has not been the biggest offender. The United States has not been a historic violator of Security Council resolutions simply because it can veto any resolution it does not like before it can reach the General Assembly for vote.

In fact, America has used its powerful Security Council veto to stop numerous globally oriented United

Nations resolutions, including a resolution to compel all countries to be bound by international law and a resolution for all countries to comply with the newly formed independent International Criminal Court (ICC). Historically, United Nations international justice courts had condemned America for illegal and violent actions in Nicaragua (see Nicaragua section).

For the most part, United States government actions at the UN Security Council have less to do with a desire for true global justice, and more to do with the exercise of American power for its own self-interests. Other examples to illustrate this point include the United States government standing alone (in some cases along with Israel) against essentially the entire world regarding the reaffirmation of a 1925 treaty banning biological weapons, and against a resolution that would have strengthened a treaty banning weapons in outer space.

Although American citizens have consistently indicated widespread support for the United Nations via polling, the American government has had changing attitudes toward the United Nations depending on the institution's willingness to support prevailing American foreign policy.

In recent years, the United States government has even withheld paying dues to the United Nations in the amount of approximately $1 billion, and some American government officials have even suggested forming a new alternative international institution that would allow as members only those countries that have adopted democratic political systems.

International Legal Courts – America has a history of resisting the creation and implementation of truly democratic-oriented international justice systems.

The United States government has resisted ratification of the establishment of the new independent International Criminal Court (ICC). Post Iraq War, the American government also pressured the United Nations for an exemption from prosecution by a new international war crimes tribunal for actions taken by American military personnel serving in Iraq.

Most recently, America has increased its demands to include an exemption for non-military as well as military American personnel. And, to exert more direct pressure, the American government eliminated military aid funding from 35 countries that would not support the unique legal exemption.

Many people suspect that the American government has opposed the establishment of proposed international criminal courts out of fear that its military and political leaders (like leaders from other nations) might be held accountable for their actions and called to answer to the court. For example, the Greek Bar Association announced that it plans to file a complaint with the ICC charging Britain's Prime Minister with war crimes and crimes against humanity in prosecuting the Iraq War.

The ICC is a credible organization in which the prosecutor for the ICC is an elected official and is currently a Harvard Law Professor from Argentina. About one half of the nations have already signed onto the ICC. And while the American government remains one of only 7 nations resisting the establishment of the ICC, the government is also attempting to eliminate one of the few other remaining forums to resolve international justice disputes. This is the long-standing sanctioned use of American courts by foreign citizens to bring legal claims against international despots and multinational corporations under the 1789 Alien Tort Claims Act.

This endangered legal forum has historically supported the enforcement of rights guaranteed under international agreements, such as the Covenant on Civil and Political Rights of which America is a party.

As a final note, American military use of cluster bombs resulted in legal action being brought before a Belgian court accusing United States General Tommy Franks and United States Colonel Brian McCoy of war crimes.

Belgian law for years claimed universal jurisdiction for war crimes, genocide, and crimes against humanity, regardless of the nationality of the accused. A number of American political and military leaders were named in lawsuits including former President George H. W. Bush, Secretary of State Colin Powell, Persian Gulf War General Norman Schwarzkopf, President George W. Bush, and Secretary of Defense Donald Rumsfeld.

Because of the threat of this legal action, the American government successfully pressured Belgium to shut down in part this alternative avenue for non-Belgians to seek international justice. The American government did this by threatening European countries with the prospect of withholding $350 million for NATO, with pulling NATO headquarters out of Belgium, and threatening to not show up for meetings if they were held in Belgium. Belgium did not have the strength to resist this extortive demand by the American government and hence capitulated to weakening their international war crimes law.

Treatment of Military Personnel – Americans join the military for a variety of reasons. For some, the motivation is a deeply held genuine loyalty to their country and a desire to serve, which they understand may eventually demand the sacrifice of their life. Others join the military because they want to take advantage of military benefits such as a paid education. For some, joining the military may be the best or only choice given their life situation. And for others, the military offers an outlet for personal aggression and ready access to military power and weapons.

By in large, newly enlisted American soldiers are for the most part young and innocent. They are indoctrinated and rigorously trained by military institutions to follow absolutely the orders of senior American military and political leaders. This latter group of people is responsible for American military action, good or bad. And, not unlike many other countries, America is a country where a wealthy elite class is protected from danger by a military force largely composed of people from a relatively poor underclass.

Although there are many cases of military and ex-military personnel content with their treatment in the United States military institution, there has historically been troubling issues surrounding the treatment of military personnel that should cause every American citizen and their elected officials to take notice and act, especially given the sacrifices that these young men and women made in service to their country.

There is a growing body of information (much of it not well-known, or even suppressed) relating to shameful treatment of American military personnel both during and after service. Examples include the exposure of soldiers to toxic wartime substances such as Agent Orange (a powerful defoliant extensively used by the United States military in Vietnam), and exposure to depleted Uranium (a substance commonly used to produce modern missiles).

There is also Gulf War syndrome (estimated to affect 300,000 of the 700,000 troops who served in that conflict), and there are military personnel who have suffered devastating effects possibly due to mandatory but essentially experimental anthrax vaccinations administered prior to the Iraq War. Many soldiers refused to accept the anthrax vaccination, and then suffered serious consequences for their position including ostracism, dishonorable discharge, and even court martial.

It is not uncommon for war veterans who complain of an unexplained sickness to be dismissed as "complainers" or "opportunists". And, although military service injuries are certainly not the only cause for homelessness, it is not uncommon today for 30% of the homeless population in any given community to be ex-military personnel.

Ironically, in the understandable outpouring of national grief following the World Trade Center attacks, the American government quickly granted huge monetary compensation awards to the families of victims of the attack, while continuing to allow scores of military veterans and their families to stand by with much less in the way of government support or compensation for their own sacrifices, the huge but often forgotten other costs of war.

Money and Democracy – (Much of the information in this section originated from the "Frontline: The Betrayal of Democracy" videodocumentary with William Greider)

By and large, America is now a country with a single political party. It's the party of the "corporate moneyed".

The typical American citizen has suspected this fact for years. There is widespread disillusionment among people regarding the political establishment's ability to respond to their day-to-day needs. The American people now acknowledge the overwhelming leverage of corporate money on the final outcome of important legislation and regulation. The people increasingly ignore the tired rhetoric from politicians that seems to bear little connection to the mainstream beliefs of American citizens.

The state of America's political system today is grim. The voice of the "people" is undeniably absent. Virtually the only voices that have a real bearing on the outcome of the political (and at times even the legal) system have been the voices of big business through their high-priced lobbying firms and lawyers.

Examples are too numerous to cite, however the following example is offered as only one example.

Americans have consistently supported the need for health care system reform. According to the Institute of Medicine, the American economy loses between $65 billion to $130 billion every year to sickness and early deaths due to uninsured persons. 41 million Americans (estimates range from 30 – 70 million, 18% of them between the ages of 16 and 65) lack health insurance. Caring for these people is estimated to cost $34 billion to $69 billion.

When the American government seriously considered health care reform in the early 1990s and proposed providing health care coverage for 41 million Americans presently uncovered, the insurance industry responded to guard their business interests by spending $100 million in political lobbying, $60 million on advertising, and by financing 350 free trips for members of Congress.

Despite this current state of affairs, America has had periods in history where the government made genuine attempts to balance big business influence on government with influence from the common American citizen. President Franklin D. Roosevelt promoted a "New Deal" with the people in order to strengthen the interests of the common American.

Ironically, while President Roosevelt's policies helped millions of Americans, they also served as a "wake up call" to private industry which felt that they must strengthen its influence on national policy by increasing lobbying efforts on politicians and insiders in Washington D.C. The upshot: Big business realized that they needed to protect their profits and markets by increasing their influence on public policy, law and industry regulation by hiring even more lobbyists, lawyers, and public relations firms to advocate their interests.

During a period of intense American social turmoil in 1969 through 1972, an activist government proactively worked to strengthen consumer rights, labor rights, and a number of other interests on behalf of the common American. This activity further accelerated private industry lobbying expenditures.

In 1971, there were less than 200 companies that had registered lobbyists in Washington D.C. By 1981, there were 2,000 such companies. It was a bonanza of big business investment into federal-level political influence. Perhaps more importantly, political influence was directed not only toward federal law, but also toward the detailed industry regulations, which arguably have an even stronger impact on the ultimate outcome of legislation. This crafting of industry regulation is a process that almost all common Americans never see, and almost certainly don't participate in. Some examples follow.

Despite consumer and labor protections won in the years leading up to 1972, by 1977, the act guaranteeing workers safety was under fire, the new agency charged with protecting consumers was prohibited from regulating cigarettes or guns, highway safety programs were curtailed, and intense pressure by auto manufacturers opened up congressional debate regarding the clean air laws enacted just 7 years earlier.

In the early 1970s, big business began to give money to and lobby Democrats, as well as their traditional Republican allies. Concurrent with this trend, campaign reform rules enacted through 1974 legislation allowed businesses to spend unlimited amount of money in the form of political action committee (PAC) funds. The money stakes exploded and by the 1990s, a member of the United States Senate who was an incumbent and running for reelection needed to raise $3,000 per day each day for 6 years. If he or she expected a difficult reelection, the bill would increase to $6,000 per day each day for 6 years.

In the current Presidential election cycle, America's President George W. Bush will spend at least $426,624 per day, seven days a week, from June 2003 to November 2004 on his reelection campaign.

The only real sources for this amount of money is big business, major political party leadership, and very wealthy individuals. Money originating from the common American citizen is barely large enough to register with astute politicians. American government has arguably become, more than at any other time in its history, a government to the highest bidder.

It is unsurprising then that elected officials focus inordinately on sources of capital, rather than sources of votes to get elected or reelected. This is because with modern communications technology such as television, money that supports political advertising literally translates to votes. Politicians can focus almost exclusively on buying media access, and they do not feel much pressure to directly meet and communicate with the American people. The result is that the common American's legitimate concerns, fears, and emotions simply no longer register with politicians in their decision making process.

Once a politician is successful in playing the money game and securing their position within this system, it becomes very comfortable and they do not want to rock the boat. It engenders an "If everyone else is doing it, how can it be wrong?" mentality and political culture. Promises made to the American public are habitually broken because usually there are few, if any, real consequences.

Politicians have also degenerated to the practice of passing what is termed "hollow laws". Hollow laws are legislation that contain no detail and are designed to give the American voter the false illusion that a problem has been fixed (when not much has been really accomplished) so that the voter will reelect their political representative. Unbeknownst to the voter, the real important detail (the enforceable rules) is determined through the process of creating specific industry regulations.

Currently, only big business and wealthy interests have the money to pay lawyers to sit through this long and arduous process in order to safeguard and expand their particular interests. During this critical regulation process, the interests of the American people are largely not represented at all. And, if the interests of common Americans are represented, they are vastly outgunned by the sheer manpower and money provided by corporate interests. As observed by one person, people come and go from the process, but big business can afford to remain at the table forever until their interests are secured.

To make matters even worse, the White House now serves as a virtually invisible "court of appeals" to big business interests. This is a forum where big business grievances with national policy may be fixed in their favor removed from the public eye. These meetings between the elected government and big business are not subject to public disclosure. The purpose is to serve ostensibly as "advisory groups" to Presidential administrations. However, their influence is much stronger than this characterization implies. These groups go by the names of the "Competitiveness Council", the "Defense Policy Board", and the "Energy Policy Board".

The American Vice President usually chairs these types of industry meetings. These groups tend to be populated largely by lifetime insiders who have bounced back and forth between public service (ex-Generals, military advisors, or federal energy policy officials), and the private sector (Military contractor CEOs, big military contractor lobbyists, or CEOs of large energy companies).

These are forums through which powerful industry influence can be further exerted on national policy outside of the eyes of the general public. And, it is likely in these forums that highly sensitive issues regarding industrial deregulation, industrial privatization, and the various stakes in domestic and international markets are likely to be discussed. This might even include markets that deal with the production and distribution of resources historically recognized as belonging to the American people. Essentially, this is a situation where the fox is guarding the henhouse.

The membership, agenda, and proceedings of these meetings are largely if not entirely undisclosed to the American public. What has been understood has largely been determined through relentless efforts of organizations specifically formed to dig out information regarding these activities.

A recent specific example is the ongoing fight by many organizations and individuals to compel disclosure relating to proceedings of the Energy Policy Board under Vice President Dick Cheney. Attention to this board has understandably increased in the wake of national deregulation of the energy industry, and the collapse of Enron Corporation. This struggle for information continues to this day.

Government was originally intended by the founders to serve the will of the American people, and as an entity empowered *by the people* to constrain the worst instincts and behaviors of the private sector. Sadly, America's government has arguably degenerated into a hired gun primarily loyal to the interests of big business, while the interests of common Americans largely cut out of the picture.

For contemporary American politicians, the question is simple. Which master should they serve? Should they serve common constituents who can't give much money, and can easily be fooled with respect to what the politician is really doing in Washington D.C. Or, should they serve large corporate interests who have large sums of money that will practically buy the politician media coverage and get him or her reelected. The practical choice becomes, if not easy, the most likely route. Furthermore, the money that is spent by politicians for reelection tends to be less to inform and educate, and more to attract attention, entertain, and invoke strong emotion.

It also used to be that people working in the news media served the interests of the people. These early reporters took pride in taking an adversarial role with respect to American government officials and big business leaders. Now, they have annual dinners with the very same politicians and business leaders that they are supposed to critique. And, to make matters worse, the media itself has become a big business, and the mainstream media message has become more uniform (a perspective on this topic is included in the Media Consolidation and Control section).

Movement Toward a Police State – Bolstered by the current climate of fear in America, the American government led by the Attorney General has continually worked to institute legal and procedural changes that in a very real way threaten America's civil liberties. Some Americans might be quite apathetic regarding the loss of civil liberties (presumably for more national security) until it affects them directly and they experience its powerful ramifications.

Government intrusion on the rights of citizens is again not new. The early American colonists knew very well the propensity of rulers and governments to expand and abuse their powers over citizens of states. They had experienced it firsthand through their dealings with England.

As a response, America's founders installed and institutionalized certain Bill of Rights specifically to protect American citizens from abusive government intrusion; really to protect democracy itself. Examples are the First (free speech and assembly), Fourth (unreasonable search and seizure), Fifth (self-incrimination and privacy), and Sixth (legal processes) Amendments to the Constitution. Recent actions by the United States Department of Justice clearly work to weaken the intent and effect of these Constitutionally protected provisions.

The following is only a sampling of the real-life manner whereby American civil liberties are seriously threatened by current trends: Disclosure of reading habits by libraries and book stores, of private telephone and email records, of financial and travel information, credit files, and other personal data. Easing of restrictions on FBI investigators. Monitoring of internet website visit logs and classes enrollment records. Infiltration of political meetings and worship services. Surveillance of phone lines and internet chat rooms. Secret searches of homes and businesses. Subpoenas that require businesses to disclose private customer information, and surveillance warrants allowing for spying of individuals and organizations without judicial review.

Other examples include the detention of people without pressing charges, encouragement of federal agencies to reject Freedom of Information Act (FOIA) requests, illegally sealing papers of former presidents, and pushing for expansion of the USA Patriot Act to provide even more surveillance and physical search powers.

Many Americans may not know of a relatively unknown legal venue in America called the Foreign Intelligence Surveillance Court (FISC) established under the 1978 Foreign Intelligence Surveillance Act (FISA). FISA was originally passed by Congress to respond to perceived threats relating to the Cold War with the Soviet Union and the growing incidence of terrorist threats, while instituting some level of review on government spying which was rampant at the FBI during the Herbert Hoover years.

FISC is a 7-judge secret court (no publicly disclosed information or close oversight, and hearings conducted in a windowless courtroom) that considers requests by the United States Justice Department and the Intelligence agencies for approval for covert surveillance and physical searches on suspected persons by a wide variety of means, many of them previously enumerated.

The court has much latitude to validate a request, even with sparse or no direct evidence. Of the over 10,000 requests that the court reviewed over a 19-year time period, none (zero) of the requests have been denied with the exception of one case in which the petitioners themselves (the FBI and NSA) requested application denial. FISC, if not in actual fact, certainly has the appearance of being a "rubber stamp" court dispensing easy-to-obtain approvals for surveillance and searches on both American citizens and non-citizens by intelligence organizations.

As a note, another secret court was established in 1995 by Congress, called the Alien Terrorist Removal Court.

Also related to the reduction of civil liberties and privacy protections was the revelation of a military project under the Secretary of Defense originally named Total Information Awareness (TIA). The TIA project was intended to advance the collection of massive amounts of electronic information on people, centralize the information on a grand database, and use the system to acquire and query information on individuals that the government deem "suspicious".

It is suggested that the reader might consider carefully all the types of information that they have stored throughout various systems in paper or electronic form, and whether they would feel comfortable if their government had easy and free access to that information.

On Weapons and Weapons-of-Mass-Destruction (WMD)

Chapter Summary – The development and proliferation of nuclear, chemical, and biological weapons during the past half century has dramatically changed the global environment in many ways, while leaving other factors largely unchanged. Military conflict has been a recurring activity from the beginnings of human history, and this fact has not changed. What has changed is that never before have humans had such a vast portfolio of powerful weapons technology with the aggregate capability to literally destroying human civilization. The reasons for war have not fundamentally changed, but the ultimate consequences of war have dramatically changed.

While it is true that this relatively new devastating weapons technology is becoming increasingly accessible to peoples around the world that are not Americans, it is also true that close inspection of the history of WMD reveals that the United States has played a seminal and pervasive role in the technology's development, proliferation, and use. And furthermore, that the rules relating to the ownership and control of WMD have been grossly inconsistent when applied globally.

The reader is also encouraged to consider the notion that conventional weapons technology used on massive scale (such as massive bombing campaigns) should really be considered a "weapon of mass destruction" because these techniques clearly and verifiably result in the immediate and long-term deaths of very large populations of people.

If WMD is viewed in this context, there are numerous examples of American mass killings in this chapter, as well as the chapters relating to Genocide and Foreign Aggression.

United States Military Spending – The United States entire budget for 2004 is about $2.2 trillion. The military portion of this budget is $400 billion, 18% of the entire budget. (This level of military expenditure does not even include additional expenses, such as for additional fuel or replacement supplies and munitions, if America were to actually execute a war plan. This is the military's ongoing "idle" cost.)

However, closer inspection of the details reveals the following: 56% of the entire budget is already designated as mandatory and predetermined spending (e.g. social security, Medicare, Medicaid and SCHIP, interest payments on existing debt). Of the remaining 44% of the entire budget that is discretionary spending (i.e. spending that we can choose), America allocates about ½ to the military.

In other words, military expenditures claim 50% of what Americans can decide to spend their money on; and the remaining money must be fought over by all the other governmental agencies. These agencies fund important societal needs and include investments into education, health and human services, transportation, labor, environment and national parks, and energy (such as investments into renewable energy development, and accelerating energy efficiency and conservation programs, which collectively would alleviate America's huge dependence on petroleum products).

Put another way, America spends most of its discretionary money preparing to fight wars, fighting wars, and healing itself and others from wars fought. This when the country is already an undisputed military and economic superpower.

To look at it from another perspective, the proposed American military budget increase (only the increase, not the military budget) in recent years has been larger than the *entire* military budget for almost every other country on this planet. No other country comes remotely close to the level of military spending by America (including Russia).

This situation is analogous to the biggest, richest, most heavily-armed child in the playground using most of his allowance to purchase more guns, at a time when almost every other child in the playground has only sticks to defend themselves against the wishes of the first child.

Furthermore, to add insult to injury, the United States military has recently acknowledged huge amounts of unaccounted spending totaling around $1 trillion. The military cannot account for 56 airplanes, 32 tanks, and 36 Javelin missile command launch units, and other military equipment.

United States as a Global Weapons Dealer – America supplies 64% of the world's weapons. This represents $33 billion out of the $52 billion total world market for arms. This is an all-time record. America sells and delivers more weapons than all other countries on the planet combined. Of the 43 countries with over $500,000 in arms imports during the years of 1997-1999, fully 23 of them obtained 2/3 or more of their weapons imports from the United States.

Highly industrialized and economically developed nations account for 96% of the weapons sold to the world. Developing and undeveloped countries essentially have no choice but to purchase defense technology (if they can afford it at all) from the much more powerful countries such as the United States, Britain, Russia, France, and Germany – countries that may not be friendly to them. This amounts to immense political leverage and advantage, particularly for the United States.

Many regions in the world have become major trading markets for weapons while massive numbers of people are killed. One example is the ongoing conflict in the Congo, which is located in southwest Africa. Most Americans are unaware that the Congo has been the site of the largest human war since World War II.

Aggressive multinational corporate interests have been involved in the Congo as the creation and adoption of mining codes will strongly influence how they will be able to profit from the natural resources in the region. There is an emerging economic picture whereby common Congolese will earn little to find precious mineral resources. They will then supply the minerals to rich armed warlords, who will then sell the valuable minerals to multinational corporate interests.

During the 1990s alone, the American government gave more than $200 million in military equipment and training to African armies, including 6 of the 7 neighboring countries involved in the Congo's bloody wars. An estimated 3.3 million Congolese, fully 7% of the population, have died in the 5-year war.

Global Nuclear Weapons Inventory - Nations that have access to nuclear weapons:

United States	10,500 warheads
Russia	20,000 warheads
	10,000 deployed
China	400 warheads
France	450 warheads
Britain	185 warheads
Israel	200 warheads (estimated)
India	65 warheads
Pakistan	30-50 warheads
North Korea	1-2 warheads (estimated)

In terms of stockpiles of nuclear raw materials, America has more than 12,000 plutonium pits in storage at the Pantex plant near Armarillo, Texas. There is nearly 200 tons of highly enriched uranium at the Oak Ridge Reservation in Tennessee.

North Korea has recently come under fire by the American government because North Korea has been developing nuclear weapons in violation of weapons treaties. North Korea has acknowledged the existence of their nuclear weapons development program.

Because America has upwards of 10,500 nuclear weapons, and has even sited and aimed some of them at North Korea, the North Korean government has sought to develop its own nuclear weapons capability to counter America's power and aggression.

The Clinton administration negotiated with North Korea regarding nuclear weapons non-proliferation, and at that time they created expectations from both the North Korean and South Korean governments involving promises of fuels supplies and American acceptance of a non-aggression pact. The subsequent Bush administration shocked both North and South Korea by quickly reversing its posture and attitude. This action not only destroyed the diplomatic advances achieved by the Clinton administration, it also jeopardized the plans by South Korea and North Korea for reunification of Korea.

Nuclear Weapons Research and Production – In a clear reversal from five decades of nuclear delegitimization and disarmament since the Cold War, and in contradiction to what the United States itself demands of other countries, the American government is in the process of approving research into additional nuclear weapons capabilities.

These projects include small-scale weapons for battlefield use (low-yield nuclear weapons), and nuclear weapons with absolutely huge explosive capability for underground bunker attacks. This latter weapon is a hydrogen-based bomb would have the destructive capability of up to 1 megaton, or six times the destructive capability of the bomb used in Hiroshima at the end of World War II.

Included in the American weapons development plan is the use of non-military sites to be used for military weapons development purposes. An example is the production of tritium at the Watts Bar nuclear reactor in Tennessee. Tritium is a material that heightens the explosive force of nuclear weapons. The United States government has also revealed a plan to produce more than 450 plutonium warhead triggers per year. These are devices that are a critical component of nuclear weapons.

The impetus for this devastating reversal in nuclear weapons policy has come largely from the Presidential administration and some members of the Congress and Senate, and not the military itself. The country already has a remaining stockpile of low-yield nuclear weapons developed in the 1950s and 1960s, and there are many other major concerns (both inside and outside of the military) relating to the use of these types of weapons.

Chemical Weapons Technology Activity – Humans have used chemical weapons for hundreds of years, if chemical weapons can be defined broadly as the use of any material that is toxic or poisonous. Examples abound, including the use of common substances such as pesticides and mercury. In World War I, mustard gas was a commonly used blister agent by soldiers as a chemical weapon. In World War II, the Nazis used the blood agent cyanide for Jewish genocide. There are choking agents such as phosgene and chlorine. Nerve agents are relatively new, are the most toxic, and include sarin, tabun, soman, GF, and VX.

Declared chemical weapons holders include the United States, Soviet Union, India, and South Korea. Old or abandoned chemical weapons holders include Belgium, France, Germany, Italy, Japan, and Britain. The United States has also left many old and abandoned chemical weapons at military bases located both domestically and internationally around the world (e.g. at a World War II American military testing facility in Panama).

In 2001, the American inventory of known chemical warfare material consisted of a 31,279 ton chemical weapons stockpile in 8 locations, and over 100 locations with non-stockpiled chemical weapons material.

One example is the Anniston Army depot in Alabama which holds approximately 2,200 tons of deadly VX and sarin nerve agents and mustard gas. The toxic chemicals are packed into upwards of 660,000 chemical weapons. The weapons are stored in concrete bunkers called "igloos" where aging mortars and M-55 rockets are already leaking toxic gas. These igloos are located in a populated area with 250,000 residents within a 30-mile radius.

In addition to the decades-long costs to produce and store the huge number of chemical weapons at the Anniston Army depot, $1 billion in additional taxpayer money has now been required to pay for the equipment to destroy the weapons. Examples of other locations where American chemical weapons stockpiles have had to be destroyed include Tooele, Utah and Johnston Atoll near Hawaii.

Despite continuing public condemnation of weapons-of-mass-destruction, the American government itself has pulled back with regards to its support of major international chemical weapons agreements such as a strengthening of the 1972 Biological and Toxin Weapons Convention (BTWC) and the 1993 Chemical Weapons Convention (CWC). This is in contradiction to the position held by most other nations.

Biological Weapons Technology Activity – America has been a primary developer of biological technology as applied to weapons. These types of weapons may cause high levels of mortality because they spread diseases that can be transmitted from person-to-person.

In the latter half of the 1900s, a number of countries (predominantly America and the Soviet Union) developed the deadly bacteria anthrax. These development activities included efforts to weaponize the anthrax. This effort consisted of manufacturing high-quality anthrax spores (small particles) of an optimum size, and creating and testing the means to deliver the material. Other devastating biological agents were studied including Botulism, Plague, Smallpox, Tularemia, and viral hemorrhagic fever (e.g. Ebola). The United States was an early leader in developing this deadly technology.

Currently, samples of Smallpox are believed to be in possession of two countries, America and the Soviet Union. Tularemia is one of the most infectious bacteria known. Tularemia was researched and developed by the America, its allies, and Japan during World War II. This was one of several biological weapons stockpiled by the United States military in the late 1960s.

Major international biological weapons agreements such as a strengthening of the 1972 Biological and Toxin Weapons Convention (BTWC) and the 1993 Chemical Weapons Convention (CWC) encountered major obstacles in 2001. The American government, in contrast to most other nations, has stalled on supporting these international treaties as drafted. This is believed to be largely because of a heightened sense of national vulnerability in America after the events of September 11.

The American government has also not moved aggressively on enacting these treaties because it has renewed it's own biological weapons activity. The United States not only has some of the largest inventories of nuclear and chemical weapons, it also has the world's largest bio-weapons program. Among known American activity (it is generally believed that there are also other unknown programs) are 3 secret biological weapons defense programs possibly already illegal under the BTWC.

It should be noted that a country does not need to have an overt offensive biological weapons program to develop biological weapons technology. Simply developing defensive biological weapons (such as exists in the United States) spawn offensive biological weapons technology as a natural outcome of the defense research.

Post Gulf War, it was revealed that the United States Army had developed batches of very fine anthrax spores, and aerosolized them (made to float through the air). The Army was also recently embarrassed by the revelation of an American Army patent for a new rifle-launched gas grenade. The patent for the device listed under its patent characteristics that the weapon can deliver chemical and biological agents. These are two payloads forbidden by international treaty and American law.

Internationally, the American government has been fearful of other nations or groups also acquiring biological weapons technology. Thus, America has offered substantial amounts of money to countries (including Eastern Bloc countries such as Uzbekistan) in order to apply strong economic pressure for their compliance with weapons treaties favored by the United States. And recently, the American government surprised many countries by accusing Iran, Iraq, Libya, North Korea, Sudan, and Syria of maintaining bio-weapons programs, while conspicuously not mentioning other nations possessing weapons-of-mass-destruction technology, including America's longtime ally Israel.

Hiroshima and Nagasaki – America remains the only nation in the world that has actually used a nuclear weapon for wartime purposes. Two weapons were discharged during World War II, primarily on Japanese non-combatants in the cities of Hiroshima and Nagasaki.

The immediate estimated civilian fatality count in Hiroshima alone was 150,000 people. The total rose to 230,000 as additional tens of thousands died of radiation poisoning in the aftermath. 74,000 people are estimated to have died immediately in the Nagasaki bombing, with additional tens of thousands of deaths in the aftermath.

As a note, during World War II, relentless massive American bombing campaigns on major Japanese cities resulted in the death of upwards of ½ million Japanese civilians. Over 80,000 civilians were killed in a single night of bombing in Tokyo. Weapons that can cause massive death and destruction are most certainly not limited to nuclear, chemical, or biological weapons.

Vietnam – During the Vietnam War from 1965 through the cease fire in 1973, massive amounts of chemical weapons were dropped into Vietnam, Cambodia, and Laos by the American military. 11 million liters (a liter is approximately equivalent to 1/4 gallon) of Agent Orange, a toxic plant defoliant, was dropped these Southeast Asian countries. In addition, the United States military dropped massive amounts of Phosphorus bombs and Napalm bombs (essentially "jellied gasoline"). The result was literally millions of civilian Vietnamese deaths.

Despite the American aura surrounding the "great war" of World War I and the "good war" of World War II, many people are unaware that in the Vietnam War America unleashed a greater tonnage of bombs than was dropped in *all* of World War II. This resulted in the estimated deaths of 1 to 3 million mostly civilian Southeast Asian people, 58,000 American military deaths, and 300,000 American military serious injuries. The

Vietnam War was an example of American use of deadly weapons on a massive scale.

Depleted Uranium – The American military commonly uses radioactive material in the form of depleted Uranium in the construction of its missiles. Depleted Uranium is used because it is both a very dense material (much more dense than even lead), and because the material burns on impact; thereby augmenting the ability of weapons to penetrate thick metal armor.

Depleted Uranium is a residual material remaining from the uranium enrichment process to make fissionable material for nuclear power (in the form of fuel rods) or for nuclear weapons. Upon impact, depleted Uranium is dispersed throughout the impact area and will remain a continuing, albeit not precisely understood, health hazard to persons exposed to the material.

The American military apparently recognizes the health hazard because it trains American soldiers on methods to protect against exposure to this toxic material. Although science indicates that this material is clearly detrimental to human health, and that there have been documented cases of human depleted Uranium contamination, the ultimate effect on civilian populations exposed to this radioactive material post war is not clearly understood.

In the 1989 Gulf War, America used an estimated 320 tons of depleted Uranium material. Estimates for the recent Iraq War have ranged from 1,000 to 2,000 tons, although these latter figures are in dispute.

Cluster Bombs – A typical cluster bomb weighs 1000 pounds and contains 250 palm-sized canisters called "bomblets" or "bombies". These bomblets are designed to explode into hundreds of fragments over an area the size of a football field. Typically when a cluster bomb is deployed, 16% (range is 5% to 20%) of the bomblets remain on the ground unexploded. These become latent time bombs to the civilian population that ultimately return to the bombed area.

Estimated direct civilian deaths due to the use of cluster bombs during the 3-week Iraq War vary from up to 200 people. It is a certainty that unexploded bomblets on the ground will be responsible for future unintended deaths or severe injuries, mainly to children who mistake the bomblets as attractive toys and disturb them.

For example, after the Gulf War in 1991, more than 1,600 Kuwaiti and Iraqi civilians were killed, 2,500 civilians were injured, and 80 American soldiers were killed by an estimated 1.2 million unexploded bomblets.

The American military has reported the use of 1,500 cluster bombs (not bomblets) in the recent Iraq operation, 26 of them were within 1,500 feet of civilian neighborhoods. It is thought that this estimate does not include the cluster bombs that were deployed though the use of rocket launchers, which can contain up to 12 cluster bombs, each containing typically 644 bomblets.

The British military has reported the use of 2,000 cluster bombs, 66 of which were dropped around the city of Basra. Both the neighborhood of Doura and cities such as Najaf has been infected with bomblets.

The American military has used cluster bombs in other previous military conflicts. For example, in the 78-day military operation in Kosovo, 1,765 cluster bombs were used resulting in 50 people killed and 101 people injured during the first year after the end of military operations alone. In Afghanistan, American military forces are estimate to have killed 127 civilians through the use of cluster bombs.

America's use of cluster bombs resulted in legal action being brought before a Belgian court accusing American General Tommy Franks and American Colonel Brian McCoy of war crimes.

Saddam Hussein's Weapons Supplier – For more than 10 years primarily during the 1980's, American companies with American government approval shipped chemicals and biological seed supplies to Iraq.

In those years, Iraq was fighting an 8-year war with Iran and the American government considered Saddam Hussein an ally to American geopolitical interests in the region. It is well known that the Iraq government used chemical weapons against the Kurds in Halabja and 50 other villages in Northern Iraq. As a result, an estimated 8,000 Kurds were massacred in 1983. Thousands of lives were devastated, and of course the likely source of weapons material was America.

Prior to the United States invasion of Iraq in March 2003, the Iraqi government submitted a 1,200 page weapons declaration document itemizing lists of western nations, corporations, organizations, and individuals who supplied Iraq with weapons technology and products. The American government tried to prevent public disclosure of this information, but information was revealed and included about 100 well-known and respected American corporations.

Among the findings with regards to weapons-of-mass-destruction supplies to Iraq, is a Maryland company that supplied thiodiglycol, a mustard gas precursor, and a

Tennessee manufacturer that supplied chemicals used for the production of sarin nerve gas.

Furthermore, the highest grades of seed-stock for anthrax germs, as well as for botulism, E. coli and other organisms were supplied to Iraq legally under official United States Department of Commerce license throughout the 1980s. In fact, Senate Banking subcommittee reports from 1994 confirmed shipments of biological germ stock to Iraq well into 1989.

Of course, being a major supplier of the deadly weapons technology during this time period, the CIA, State Department, and the United States military were very aware of Iraq's growing biological weapons capabilities. A mere 6 months after Iraq's genocidal use of chemical weapons in Halabja, an American company sent 11 strains of germs to Iraq. This shipment included 4 types of anthrax, including a microbe strain called 11966 developed specifically for germ warfare by the United States military at Fort Detrick in Maryland during the 1950s.

One might conclude from this history that the American government believes it morally acceptable to use weapons-of-mass-destruction on people, so long as the American government is the institution that determines who is slaughtered by them.

Military Research Grants – Every year, large amounts of American taxpayer money is given to research organizations and private companies to envision and develop technologies that are intended to advance American military capability or to strengthen national security.

Grants come in many forms. They can be awarded directly from a branch of the armed services, or they can be awarded through another venue (either publicly known or covert) such as the Defense Advanced Research Projects Agency (DARPA) operating within the Defense Secretary's office with a $3 billion annual budget.

Examples of historical beneficiaries of DARPA taxpayer money have been the major technology labs such as Lawrence Berkeley Laboratory, Lawrence Livermore Laboratory, Los Alamos National Laboratory, and other well known and also lesser known technology companies.

Some of the technologies that were funded by American taxpayer money (many were subsequently turned over to private industry to generate private sector commercial profit) include the M-16 rifle, the B-2 stealth bomber and F-117 tactical fighter, the unmanned Global Hawk and Predator Unmanned Vehicle, the internet, and various forms of information data mining software.

DARPA is presently pursuing expensive and complex national development projects such as an ultra-high speed armed drone that would be capable of traveling very quickly internationally to launch attacks, and a computerized system that would be capable of monitoring and recording virtually all sensory experiences of a person.

DARPA has also been involved with a controversial program originally named Total Information Awareness. This project was conceived as a sweeping electronic information system that would access diverse computer databases to collect credit, financial, medical and travel records in order to provide confidential information to government authorities on American citizens in the interest of national security.

In July 2003, the Pentagon admitted and defended the fact that DARPA had also been working on a bizarre (and arguably perverted) new project. The project was to create and establish a stock-market style system (betting parlor) which would allow investors to bet real money on the occurrence of assassinations, government coups, terror attacks, and other political events in the Middle East. A trained economist would recognize this type of system as a "futures contracts market" for Middle East events, or an investor's market for death. The Pentagon justification for this project was to possibly improve terrorist intelligence and to gain useful predictions for attacks.

There was immediate and vociferous outrage voiced by the public and from members of Congress, which forced the Pentagon to immediately terminate the ill-conceived project and led to the resignation of one of DARPA's chiefs, an ex-Admiral convicted of lying to Congress in the Iran-Contra Affair (for a brief discussion of this incident, see the Nicaragua section).

However, the revelation of this project and the question of why it was supported by the Pentagon up until the American public knew about its existence clearly left many in America questioning the mentality and morality of the United States administration and it's national security and military establishment.

On Terrorism, Torture, Genocide, and Ethnic Cleansing

Chapter Summary – Historically, America has been directly and indirectly linked to more terrorism, torture, genocide, and ethnic cleansing than its citizens may realize or care to acknowledge. The typical American pictures terrorism as represented by a person with a bomb. And, in general, the typical American view has been that terrorism, genocide, torture, and ethnic cleansing are things that happen in other countries, and certainly not in America or by Americans.

However, a careful study of American history indicates the contrary. The United States has participated in all of these derided practices. At times it has been perpetrated through direct American government action. At other times it has been through indirect action (using intermediaries, or through military or financial support of violent and brutal foreign regimes), or even through deliberate inaction.

On occasion, the activity was publicly known because of direct engagement or intervention by American forces (military, paramilitary, local law enforcement, vigilante groups, or intelligence organizations). However, in many cases the activity was covert (secret) government activity, or the activity was in the form of targeted strategic military or economic financial aid.

Because of its wealth and power, America has immense potential to do both enormous good and enormous bad. It affects the world through its actions, and its inaction. It affects the world through its foreign policy, and its domestic policy. It affects the world through its laws, its culture, and its customs. It affects the world through its prejudices, and its ignorance.

Terrorism is defined in the dictionary as "the political use of violence or intimidation". Operating under this definition, it is indisputable that America has had a long history of using terrorism to advance its national interests, and often terrorism with religious overtones. And, embedded within this history are also the common accompanying practices of genocide, ethnic cleansing, and even torture.

The numbers are staggering. People killed, tortured, terrorized, and global refugees created through direct or indirect American involvement (and based only on the specific events described in this book alone) easily reach into the millions.

What is also not commonly known by most Americans is that numerous studies regarding religious fundamentalism have concluded that America is one of the most religiously fundamentalist nations in the world, comparable to countries such as Iran and even pre-industrial societies.

In these studies, religious fundamentalism was determined by asking questions relating to beliefs in God and the Devil, religious miracles and resurrection, and belief or disbelief in scientific-based theories such as evolution. The numbers exhibited by the American populace could not even be duplicated anywhere else in the industrialized world.

If one accepts this data, America is arguably the largest, richest, most militarily powerful religious fundamentalist country in the world. This may be one of the reasons why much of the world actually views the United States as the biggest threat to global security.

American Indians – From the first days of its history and throughout the 1800s, America embarked on an aggressive and relentless expansion of its territories. After the American Revolution, the country acquired more territories of the North American continent: First, through the Louisiana Purchase by Thomas Jefferson essentially doubling the size of the nation, and then through a War with Mexico.

Throughout this expansionist period, it is estimated that upwards of 10 million native born American Indians were systematically killed through military attack, European diseases, decimation of native lands and food supplies, relocation to poor reservation lands, and poverty and starvation. This occurred at a time when the total European-American population was only about 20 million people. Using this data, one-third of the population of the people in the territories of what is now known as America were systematically annihilated.

During the early 1800s, Andrew Jackson rampaged throughout Florida virtually destroying the native population and securing control of land from the Spanish. In 1818, United States President John Quincy Adams commended Jackson's expansionist campaign for using "salutary efficacy" of terror in dealing with the "mingled hordes of lawless Indians and Negroes". This is but a single example of a long list of European-American terror actions inflicted on the native Indian and black populations throughout the expansionist time period of American history.

The first American Secretary of Defense General Henry Knox, voiced his belief that what was being perpetrated on the native populations, the destruction of the people, was worse than what the Spanish Conquistadors perpetrated in Mexico and Peru.

While in office, President John Quincy Adams founded and promoted a concept referred to as "manifest destiny". Manifest Destiny was a belief that white settlers of European ancestry were innately superior to all other races, and that they were endowed with a God-given right to annex land and to rule and "civilize" the heathen non-white people.

After President Adams left power, he came to oppose slavery and the actions toward the Indians. Adams described his involvement, along with those of his peers, as a crime of "extermination" of such enormity that God would surely punish them for these "heinous sins". It is grossly ironic that given its history with the Indians, the United States government names its modern day weapons after these early American victims of genocide (such as the Apache, Chinook, Tomahawk, and Iroquois missiles).

It could be credibly argued that America's early national wealth, which was generated through the ability of its citizens to settle lands and access natural resources to cultivate agriculture, to raise livestock, and to establish commercial enterprises was built squarely on a foundation of ethnic cleansing and genocide.

Lynching of African Americans – From the nation's earliest days, persons of African ancestry were subjected to continual and sometimes extremely violent terrorism by both the American government and its citizens.

Many of these brutal attacks were planned, organized and executed by the Ku Klux Klan, a southern organization established by a confederate officer of the Civil War, Nathan Bedford Forrest. During the organization's most active periods in American history, in the late 1800's and early 1900's, recurring intense physical and mental terrorism was perpetrated against African Americans. This included the common practices of firebombing houses, and hanging black victims on trees.

Tuskegee experiment – In 1932, 399 African Americans, many of whom were poor Alabama sharecroppers, were recruited by the United States Public Health Service (PHS) ostensibly to receive free treatment for "bad blood".

The true intent of the government's recruitment and treatment experiment was not revealed for 40 years. Unknown to the patients, the PHS was studying the effects of advanced stage syphilis, and the doctors were most interested in what could be learned by conducting autopsies on the patients after they died.

A total of 128 men died directly of syphilis or of related complications, which might include tumors, heart disease, paralysis, blindness, and insanity. 40 of the patient's wives contracted the disease, and 19 of their children had been born with congenital syphilis.

What is most shocking is that a persistent and concerted effort was made by PHS to continue to deny treatment to these human "guinea pigs". The PHS got patients exempted from military service during World War II because routine blood testing of recruits would reveal syphilis and require treatment. And, even after a highly effective cure for syphilis was discovered in the 1940s, penicillin was deliberately withheld from the patients.

Treatment of Conscientious Objectors– During World War II, hepatitis experiments were performed on people registered as "conscientious objectors"; people who refused to fight in the war for personal or religious reasons. These people were not informed of the consequences of hepatitis infection. The result was predictably illness and death.

South Korea – After World War II, the United States military entered South Korea and dissolved a budding popular anti-facist government composed largely of Koreans that had resisted the prior Japanese occupation. This action inaugurated a period of brutal repression.

Using Japanese facist police and Koreans that had collaborated with the Americans during the Japanese occupation, about 100,000 people were murdered during the late 1940s and prior to the beginning of what Americans know as the Korean War. From the American government's perspective, this mass murder was done to impede or halt the spread of communism. In one specific incident, 40,000 people were killed after the beginning of a peasant revolt on Cheju Island, a small island located off of the southern coast of South Korea.

Guatemala – During the late 1940s and early 1950s there was a popular rebellion against non-democratic rule in Guatemala, and a democratic government came to power. In 1954 the American government, through the CIA, engineered a coup to overthrow the democratically elected Guatemalan President Jacobo Arbenz and the popular movement.

This inaugurated a brutal military regime in Guatemala. In the ensuing years from 1960 through

1996, further attacks were conducted by the Guatemalan military regime to suppress what they considered to be "leftist rebel activity" and to squelch popular support for them among the common Guatemalan population.

The Guatemalan government embarked on an all-out war against the rebels from 1981 through 1982. The army systematically massacred tens of thousands of largely unarmed Guatemalan civilians, most of them Mayan Indians. The end result was an estimated 200,000 deaths (mass executions, murder, with rape and torture) of Mayan Indians during the country's brutal genocide. It has also been estimated that 50,000 other Guatemalans are missing, and that the conflict ultimately created 1.5 million refugees.

While the genocide occurred in Guatemala, the American military was providing training to a number of Guatemalan military officers regarding rebel suppression tactics. Weapons and money was provided, and the American CIA even created a clandestine radio station to help accomplish its Guatemalan regime objectives. This long, brutal suppression of the Guatemalan resistance movement and the genocide of its people continued largely because of regular intervention by the administrations of President John F. Kennedy and Lyndon Johnson.

Related to these events is the fact that post-World War II, the American military and intelligence community had a keen interest to take advantage of the acquired skills of Nazis who had practical expertise regarding the suppression of anti-facist resistance movements.

To this aim, as it became untenable for many ex-Nazis to remain in Europe, many of them were sent to the United States or even to areas such as Guatemala in Latin America to serve as military advisors to American-backed military police regimes. Some of these brutal regimes were themselves modeled on the Nazi Third Reich. Some of these same notorious ex-Nazis also eventually became drug dealers, weapons merchants, terrorists, and instructors of torture techniques originally developed by the Nazi Gestapo.

One specific example of an ex-Nazi recruited by the American government post-World War II is Klaus Barbie, a notorious and brutal Nazi SS officer and ex-Gestapo chief in France during the war. Klaus Barbie was initially recruited by the American Army to aid the United States to spy on people believed to be French-communists.

El Salvador – For years, America installed and supported dictators in El Salvador that committed torture, repression, and murder against natives that would not support American business interests. This is not well known because the American media did not highlight these events as important news.

In 1932, El Salvador experienced a popular uprising that threatened the military government, and thus America's business interests. America sent a cruiser and two destroyers that stood by while the Salvadorian government slaughtered 30,000 people.

In the 1970s, peasants in El Salvador began to develop grassroots organizations that led to more real democracy in the country, but also threatened existing American business interests. In the 1980s, the Salvadorian government launched an attack on the peasants. 600 civilian peasants, and other people who helped them, were butchered and drowned by Honduran and Salvadorian military troops, in part funded and supported by the United States.

Collectively during the years of 1946 through 1979, American military aid to El Salvador totaled approximately $17 million. In the first year of President Ronald Reagan's administration alone, the amount exploded to $82 million.

A brutally murderous Salvadorian special elite force called the Atlacatl Battalion was created, trained, and equipped by American forces. Military forces in El Salvador even forced poor teenagers to become soldiers, and trained them in Nazi SS torture and terrorist techniques. A well-known Catholic Archbishop and peasant leader, Oscar Romero, implored President Jimmy Carter to halt American aid for the Salvadorian military. The following month, the Archbishop was assassinated.

In 1980, the Salvadorian death toll was 10,000 people and quickly rose to 13,000 by 1981, spinning off an additional estimated 1 million political refuges. By 1981, the independent press in El Salvador was effectively destroyed because of the assassination of one editor, and the fleeing of another. Salvadorian witnesses who sought protection in America but faced the threat of possible deportation, have been largely silenced by the American government.

By in large, these events were not covered in the American media. When an American journalist Raymond Bonner continued his reporting on the events in El Salvador, and reported on America's relationship to the atrocities, the New York Times removed him from his reporting assignment. Bonner reported on a massacre of hundreds of Salvadorian civilians in El Mozote by a battalion of soldiers trained by America. This massacre was dismissed by the American government, but was subsequently confirmed by a United Nations Commission.

East Timor – This small island country north of Australia and between the Indian and Pacific Oceans in Southeast Asia was home to an ancient civilization. However, the land was also in close proximity to important shipping and submarine lanes, and large potential oil reserves.

Shortly after a civil conflict finally freed the natives from Portuguese control, the Indonesian government invaded the newly independent country of East Timor in 1975 and slaughtered approximately 200,000 natives (roughly one quarter of the population) and many international journalists.

Indonesia's President was a man by the name of Suharto who was an anti-Communist dictator. He came to power through a 1965 American-supported political takeover. Since that time, he was supported by the United States government in the form of over $1 billion of American weapons and aid.

The United States President requested that the Indonesian government not invade East Timor until he left the country after a diplomatic visit to Indonesia. Not only did the American government allow this genocide to happen, American companies supplied 90% of the weapons for the invasion and continued to supply additional weapons as the genocide continued. During this time period, again the major American media coverage for this event was virtually non-existent. Reporting was initially primarily from independent media organizations.

After the genocide in 1978, East Timor refugees came out of hiding in the jungles. The murder continued on suspected intellectuals and political opponents. Much of the balance of East Timor natives (total population was approximately 700,000) died through starvation. In 1990 because of intense domestic and international pressure regarding human rights atrocities in East Timor, the American government finally halted its aid to the Indonesian military

Since this horrific event, the United States administration has attempted to find a way to restore American military aid to Indonesia. Recently, the American government offered training to the Indonesian Army.

Vietnam, Cambodia, and Laos – America's involvement in Southeast Asia has arguably been one of the longest and darkest chapters in American military history and foreign policy. This war, more than any other American war, revealed the dark side of American military intervention. Thus the conflict deeply divided Americans. And, in the process, 1 to 3 million mostly civilian Southeast Asians were slaughtered with millions more dying in the aftermath due to effects of the war.

For centuries, Vietnam had fought for its independence from the Chinese and Japanese (1/4 of Vietnam's population died in a famine during this time period). Vietnam also fought for its independence from France; a brutal occupation that benefited French multinational companies including those in the rubber business. Finally, Vietnam had to even fight the Americans for its independence, unification, and sovereignty.

It was during the 1950s that the United States government felt threatened by Vietnam's growing independence, largely because there was a growing mania in America's government against the dreaded global spread of communism.

Up to the late 1960s, the American government essentially blocked any attempt at a peaceful political solution for Vietnam. And during this dark history, the American government not only subverted the only free elections in the history of Laos because the winner was not sympathetic to the United States, but America also blocked credible elections in Vietnam because there was a real probability that the popular victor of a free election was not a person approved by the United States.

American involvement in Vietnam actually began in 1955 as a simple deployment of American military advisors to counter a wildly popular effort to purge Vietnam of foreign occupiers, win its independence, and unify all provinces of Vietnam.

The Vietnamese leader during this time period was a remarkable man by the name of Ho Chi Minh. By all accounts, Ho Chi Minh was a talented Vietnamese man who was foremost a nationalist with an intense desire to unify the Vietnamese people, and secondly a supporter of Communist ideology. America has historically vilified and demonized many foreign leaders of this type (for example, Fidel Castro who lead the independence movement and unified Cuba) simply because these leaders resisted American domination and wanted to control and allocate their country's resources for their own people.

After World War II, America publicly supported the Vietnam independence movement. In the north, Ho Chi Minh brought together various factions of Vietnamese and consolidated power, while still trying to rid the north of the Chinese presence. However, in the south, the French held onto power with the help of the British.

In order to secure French support to help rid the north of the Chinese, Ho Chi Minh entered into an agreement with France that accepted French rule for a short time period, followed by a promised unified and independent Vietnam. The French reneged on their promise, and the Vietnam conflict began between the northern and southern French territories of Vietnam.

In the south, a Vietnamese government with popular support struggled against French forces for control, and the American government sent aid to the oppressive French forces. Thus, the Vietnamese war had became a global conflict in which China and Russia supported the Vietnamese people to gain reunification and independence, while an American-backed France pushed to continue its foreign rule. To Vietnamese peasants, Ho Chi Minh was a powerful and successful nationalist leader. To the American government, Ho Chi Minh was a dangerous arm of communist China and Russia.

In short, the American government was willing to deny 8 million Vietnamese a peaceful transition to a popularly supported, unified, and independent Vietnam so that the American government would feel more secure regarding the possible spread of communism.

After World War II, President Harry Truman made the first installment of direct military aid to the French in the amount of $10 million. By 1950, the American government had upped their aid to $150 million, including weapons and Napalm. By 1953, the United States government was paying 80% of the costs of this new international war, amounting to more than $1 billion per year.

Still, largely because of the high level of popular support among common Vietnamese people for unification and independence, America and France were losing its battle to subjugate the Vietnamese.

For various reasons, the Chinese and Russian governments urged the Vietnamese resistance groups to accept a plan from France that would deliver to the Vietnamese people a free general election and reunification in 2 years. By this time, the American government had given France over $2 billion to fight its Vietnam War. France, however, was worn down and began to pull away from the conflict.

The American government continued to persevere in pursuing its geopolitical interests in Vietnam. They counseled their South Vietnamese puppet regime, which was led by a brutal tyrant, to launch a massive public relations campaign in order to win popular support over Ho Chi Minh from the common Vietnamese people and even the South Vietnamese military which itself wanted the puppet regime out of power. These efforts largely failed, so the South Vietnamese regime refused the Vietnamese people the promised free general elections. This action was taken with American government concurrence and support.

The South Vietnamese regime utilized a secret police and became even more brutal. With the help of American advisors, enemies and suspected civilian sympathizers were tortured (electric shock, hanging, and needles inserted under fingernails). It was in this oppressive environment that a new South Vietnamese resistance group formed (the National Liberation Front) which became commonly known as the Viet Cong.

Oppression by the American-backed South Vietnamese government was so brutal that even common South Vietnamese, including elderly and children, staged their own spontaneous uprisings without even the participation of either the North Vietnamese military or Viet Cong. Many Americans might recall unforgettable video and photographs from this time period showing a

South Vietnamese officer executing a suspected Viet Cong sympathizer in the middle of a street with a gruesome single shot to the head.

Vietnamese Buddhists even joined in protest of the murders by the secret police forces. In another memorable incident broadcast by the American news media, a monk sat in the middle of a street and set himself on fire. Even ordinary South Vietnamese students joined the Buddhists in protests.

At the time, American President John F. Kennedy needed something to strengthen his domestic popularity because of his recent failures including the Bay of Pigs, the Russian Premier Krushchev meeting, and the erection of the Berlin Wall by the Soviet Union. The war in Vietnam became one effort that could powerfully define his presidency and garner popular domestic support.

By this time, America was spending $1.5 million per day, and had 16,000 "advisor/soldiers" in Vietnam. The American-backed South Vietnamese regime was still unsuccessful at securing popular support from the Vietnamese people. So, the American government forced the leaders of the puppet regime to flee, which they did and were eventually murdered.

The United States government, through CIA activity, supported a South Vietnamese military attack on North Vietnam. Shortly after the attack, the North Vietnamese military retaliated with an attack on an American destroyer in the Gulf of Tonkin, a seaway off the coast of Vietnam. The American government depicted this attack as unprovoked, and responded with the start of massive bombing in Vietnam. The American government fabricated and announced a second Gulf of Tonkin incident. Through these incidents, the President gained popular domestic support for American military action in Vietnam

In this manic political environment of fear in America relating to the spread of communism, a resolution was revived and passed by the United States Congress that gave the President the power to make war without a formal declaration of war. (There are startling similarities to the handling of wartime presidential powers in the events leading up to the Iraq War in the Iraq section.)

This Congressional action ushered in full American military engagement in Vietnam. A continuing serious of covert provocative attacks by the United States prompted retaliatory attacks on American forces, which then served to further fuel America's war fever. By this point in time, 200,000 American troops were in Vietnam. Many of these early troop deployments were kept secret.

America's sunk investment, and thus its commitment, to the Vietnam war continued to grow. The American government then even attempted to bribe Ho Chi Minh into submission by offering him a hydroelectric dam which would provide electricity to the Vietnamese people, but the North Vietnamese leader understandably refused to give up Vietnamese reunification and independence for a dam.

Back in America, President John F. Kennedy had been assassinated, and Lyndon B. Johnson became America's president. Shortly after being sworn into office, President Johnson staged a deliberately publicized cabinet level debate on matters relating to America's involvement in Vietnam in which he had already reached his decisions. Top administration officials framed the options to the President in a manner such that America's ego, pride and world standing would most certainly suffer irreparable damage if America withdrew from the war in Vietnam. President Johnson did not want to become the first American President to lose a war.

No debate regarding this same matter occurred in Congress because of the previously mentioned Congressional resolution ceding war powers to the President. And no troop deployment increases were announced to the American public, because the American government did not want the escalation of war to be highly-publicized and thus open to questioning and dissent.

President Johnson continued to sell the American people that their country was in Vietnam to fulfill an American promise to protect a beaten and battered people from being invaded by Communists. In his sales message, honorable and selfless Americans were depicted as fighting the evil North Vietnamese Army (NVA) and Viet Cong for Vietnamese freedom. By 1965, 500,000 American troops were in Vietnam. United States General Curtis LeMay said that "America should bomb Vietnam back to the stone age."

During the Vietnam War, which included secret bombings of neighboring Cambodia and Laos, the American military unleashed a greater tonnage of bombs than was dropped in all of World War II including massive chemical weapons such as Agent Orange, Phosphorus bombs, and Napalm. These military campaigns resulted in the deaths of 1 to 3 million mostly civilian Southeast Asian people, 58,000 American military deaths, and over 300,000 American military serious injuries. And, wherever the American military traveled in this country, villagers were relocated or slaughtered whole, villages were burned, and farm animals were destroyed.

This 18-year involvement in Southeast Asia cost American taxpayers about $150 billion dollars. 2.5 million Americans served in Vietnam, and the war left the country with about 2 million war veterans. And, as mentioned, the losses due to the genocide in the Southeast Asian countries of Vietnam, Cambodia, and Laos were virtually incalculable.

One American Vietnam war veteran who saw front line action said that he came to realize that he had become what he hated the most from his own studies of early American history. He had become the American equivalent in Vietnam of the British Redcoats in America. He was party to a military force sent into Vietnam to forcibly put down an independence and freedom movement.

Throughout this conflict, China, Russia, and the Vietnamese actively sought a peaceful political solution, but the United States government decided to continue with its massive bombings and violent attacks. However, America was continuing to lose the war in Vietnam. The American military failed in numerous attempts to shut down the Ho Chi Minh trail, an important network of supply lines from the north to the south which also weaved through Cambodia and Laos.

Eventually 20,000 North Vietnamese troops moved south to engage in what became known as the Tet (Vietnamese New Year) offensive. In 1968, for the first time, the North Vietnamese military launched a major attack in the urban area of Saigon, instead of restricting its battles to countryside guerilla fighting.

Ultimately, the North Vietnamese troops failed to liberate the south, but many important South Vietnamese sites were successfully attacked and the offensive had a strong negative effect among American public opinion for the Vietnam War. Reports of American atrocities began to emerge, including an event in the South Vietnamese hamlet of My Lai, where hundreds of Vietnamese civilians (including elderly, and women with children and infants) were rounded up, marched into a ditch, and slaughtered by American troops in 1968. It was reported that people were diving onto one another in the ditch, trying to protect loved ones and children.

The American military tried to cover up the event of My Lai, the American media largely ignored the event , while the media throughout the world reported the horrors as the evidence continued to emerge. A post-massacre American Army investigation revealed mass graves filled with largely elderly men, women, and children. Many Americans understandably believed that the events of My Lai were only unique in detail; that these types of American atrocities were occurring throughout Vietnam. Only one American military officer served any time for the My Lai atrocity. He served only 3 years under house arrest and was released under probation.

In America, public pressure mounted for the American government to withdraw from Vietnam. American television reports and video largely contradicted the optimistic reports originating from the military public relations department and the President. Support within the Johnson administration, and American popular support for the war crumbled.

A slow gradual American withdrawal of troops began to occur, but talking and negotiating went on for five more years. However, while talks were occurring during 1970 through 1975, the American government continued its genocide with massive largely secret bombing campaigns in Cambodia, a previously peaceful and geographically beautiful country. To give additional perspective, in 1971 alone 800,000 tons of bombs were dropped by American forces on Vietnam, Cambodia, and Laos.

The American CIA estimated that upwards of 600,000 Cambodians were killed during this time period of American bombing and American-sponsored conflict. Also, because critical civilian infrastructure was destroyed, American officials predicted that an additional 1 million Cambodians would eventually die through starvation and disease.

In part, because of this violent and devastated climate, peasant support grew for a political party called the Khmer Rouge. During this period of relentless American genocide, there was little American press coverage regarding the Khmer Rouge.

After 1975, the Khmer Rouge continued the stream of violence, murder and atrocities that began with the devastating massive bombings by the American military. The CIA estimated continuing Cambodian civilian casualties of 50,000 to 100,000, with an expectation of 1 million additional follow-on deaths.

It was only at this point that a massive amount of American media attention was finally focused on the genocide that had been occurring in Cambodia for years under American involvement. However, this genocide was now highly publicized because it was the evil Khmer Rouge committing atrocities under the moniker of "The Killing Fields". And ironically, while the American media trumpeted the atrocities of the Khmer Rouge, it was reporting virtually nothing regarding the genocide occurring at the same time in East Timor (for more details regarding this incident and American involvement, see the East Timor section).

Laos was also a neighboring country to Vietnam, arguably one of the poorest countries in the world at the time. In Laos, the American CIA had installed a right wing government that was facing a low-level social rebellion. The American government supported a South Vietnamese invasion of Laos and began CIA-orchestrated covert massive bombing campaigns of the country.

Afghanistan – The United States government ratified a treaty in 1994 titled the "Convention Against Torture and Other Cruel, Inhuman or Degrading Treatment or Punishment" which essentially prohibited the use of torture under any circumstances.

In apparent violation to provisions in this treaty, according to a report by the Washington Post, prisoners held at Bagram Air Force base, an American-controlled facility in Afghanistan, were subjected to treatment by American forces, the CIA, and the FBI in a manner that clearly deviated from the treaty's principles. It has been reported that prisoners were beaten, blindfolded, bound in painful "stress" positions, and subjected to days of interrogation and sleep deprivation.

As an alternate process, the United States government has turned over prisoners to law enforcement agencies in Syria, Jordan, Egypt, Morocco, and Saudi Arabia that are known to have used torture in their interrogation practices. The American government than received information back from these governments. One unnamed American official was quoted as saying, "We don't kick the [expletive] out of them. We send them to other countries so they can kick the [expletive] out of them."

An early release of a new documentary has been seen widely outside of America (including the British Parliament), but to date remains virtually unknown by the American public. The film documents disturbing events in Afghanistan indicating that the United States Special Forces and military were complicit in the gross treatment and eventual massacre of 3,000 prisoners captured in Afghanistan.

According to the documentary, fighters in Afghanistan that had surrendered to Northern Alliance and American troops under assurances that they would not be harmed, were transported in extremely cramped conditions in sealed cargo containers for up to four days in the heat of Afghanistan. When prisoners complained that they could not breath, Northern Alliance soldiers , who were the American military allies in the bombing campaigns in Afghanistan, shot bullets into packed cargo containers to create ventilation holes so that the prisoners could breath. Of course, in the process prisoners were killed.

Most of the prisoners in the cargo containers arrived at their destination dead due to suffocation, injury, or dehydration. The documentary further reports that, with knowledge and guidance by American forces and intelligence representatives, the container trucks were redirected to another site where the remaining live prisoners were summarily executed and buried with the already dead in mass graves.

Thus far, the documentary has had little showing in the United States. Reportedly, a journalist asked a senior member of the American State Department why the atrocity story had not run in any of the major American media. The spokesman replied, "You have to understand, we're involved, we're in touch with the national (newspapers) on a daily basis. This story won't run, even if it's true."

Journalists associated with the documentary, which includes an ex-BBC Television award-winning journalist, are calling for a thorough investigation of the possible war crime, and the protection of and investigation into the site of the mass graves. Two of the witnesses in the documentary have since been reportedly murdered.

Western Hemisphere Institute for Security Cooperation (WHINSEC) – This is a United States Army facility located at Fort Benning, Georgia. This institution originally began in Panama under the name of the *School of the Americas*, and it has been operated by the American military to provide training to military, law enforcement, and civilians from other countries, and to promote the democratic doctrine.

Under increasing local political pressure to leave Panama, the School of the Americas eventually moved to Georgia. However, through the relentless work of activists (many of whom are Christian religious leaders) exposing and protesting the obvious controversial nature of the organization's activities, Congress killed the School of the Americas in 2000.

However, at the same time another provision was inserted into Congressional legislation in 2001 to rebirth the institution as WHINSEC, although it has been claimed by some military personnel that the new institution has no relationship to the old institution. Since then, new legislation has been reintroduced to again shut down the institution. Unfortunately, this legislation has been held back in committee and unavailable for a vote by the larger body of Congressional legislators (see Money and Democracy section).

Programs at WHINSEC and the previously named School of the Americas have included training for counter-insurgency paramilitaries. Put another way, this is the military school where the American military trains people from other countries on techniques for suppressing people in those other countries who dare to rebel against the current American-backed civil authority.

A hypothetical analogy would be, for example, a training facility located in England during the 1700s to train American colonists on techniques that they can use on fellow colonists to help the British suppress the American Revolution. This would include providing training on specific methods to stop the work of their leaders (such as Paul Revere, Thomas Jefferson, Benjamin Franklin, John Adams, and George Washington).

The institution and its predecessor, the School of the Americas, has graduated about 60,000 Latin American soldiers. The institution has supplied references to torture manuals. Other material has been taught that are related to kidnapping, terror, and assassination.

Some of the worst human rights violators, murderers, and tyrants (e.g. the military regime responsible for the murder of 6 Jesuits, their housekeeper and her daughter in El Salvador in 1989) have received training at this facility funded by American taxpayer dollars.

Latin America will likely become an even more important geographic area to the American government, as the northern part of the continent is rich in petroleum resources.

On Capitalism and Global Resources

Chapter Summary – Rightly or wrongly, America has had a profound impact on the global distribution of wealth and world culture. This has been accomplished through the day-to-day activities of many institutions. The military institution, the multinational corporations that operate globally, the ubiquitous media, and the various international trade, financing, and diplomatic institutions all play a role in the allocation of global resources.

Although a staunch capitalist might be inclined to bask in the glow of America's economic success as unqualified proof of the righteousness of the capitalistic doctrine, the truth is that historically capitalism in America has led to a mixed bag of outcomes. It is true that as a nation, America is undeniably wealthy. However, it has also been demonstrated that American capitalism has been a duel-edged sword: A powerful engine that can do incredible good, and one just as powerful that can also do incredible bad.

America has prospered enormously throughout its relatively short history because of a number of factors. These factors would include the accumulation of wealth by conquering and annexing other territories and nations, wealth generated through the institution of African American slavery, wealth created because of the energies and ambitions of both early citizens and new (sometimes exploited) immigrants, and wealth generated through the capitalistic-based principles under which America operates.

The net effects of capitalism on America have depended on important decisions regarding where and how the practice of capitalism was applied within the broader context of the American economy, legal system, and culture. For purposes of common ownership of critical resources and establishing safeguards against very real capitalistic abuse, some sectors of the American economy have required a level of close regulation and oversight in order to protect the interests of common American citizens.

Recent experiments in deregulation (banking, telecommunications, energy, and the media) have led to mixed results, but clearly in many cases it has been absolutely devastating. Recent experience has reestablished credibility to the argument that the exercise of constraint on business activity by the people (through their government, or through other institutions and activities accountable to the people) is still is a good idea.

Embedded into this economic situation has been an underlying seismic shift in the rules relating to the global labor market. New communications technologies and the rise in global capitalism has allowed large and wealthy multinational corporations to source both their blue-collar and white-collar labor overseas to reduce costs, boost profitability, and compete globally, and to likewise market and sell their goods and services in even more disparate markets.

Therefore, American citizens, as well as citizens of other nations, face legitimate concerns regarding their respective country's ability to provide adequate jobs for their own citizens in the long run. The once-popular belief that American workers would successfully and naturally retrain and transition to more sophisticated better paying jobs while more American jobs moved offshore in greater numbers, has been discredited.

These powerful recent global trends have profoundly impacted negatively America's middle class. Recent experience has re-infused middle-America with a belief that human concerns and environmental concerns are just as important, if not more so, as bottom line financial concerns. It is in this global context that new concepts of capitalism are emerging explicitly valuing a broader variety of both non-financial and financial results.

Wealth Distribution in America and the World – Most Americans sense without being told that the America is increasingly becoming a two-tiered class system.

At the top are immensely wealthy individuals who are, in general, experiencing rapid increases in wealth and decreasing taxes. Below them in financial terms is a vanishing breed of middle class Americans experiencing a mixed bag of income and tax changes. This is followed by a rapidly growing population of citizens who have low incomes and low wealth and are experiencing higher expenses and reductions in their financial income and supports. These trends are occurring while the American economy, as well as other economies around the world, become more uncertain and unstable as jobs continually rush to the latest lowest wage country.

In financial terms, what has happened in America and across the world has resulted in an inherently unstable state-of-affairs reflected by the following startling statistics:

- The wealthiest 1% of America's population own more wealth than the bottom 95% combined.

- In 1998, Bill Gates of Microsoft as a single person, owned $46 billion in wealth. This is an amount of wealth that is larger than the *combined* total wealth of the bottom 45% of Americans. This is equivalent to 126 million American citizens.

- The wealthiest 10% of Americans own 73% of wealth of the country.

- 10% of Americans live at a poverty income level with 41 million (including 8 million children) living without basic medical care insurance.

- During the 1990s the average income of the 400 wealthiest taxpayers nearly quadrupled, while this same group experienced a sharp reduction in their capital gains tax burden (28% to 20%) over the same time period. Recent tax cut legislation has further reduced this tax burden to 15%.

- The top 200 global corporations control 27% of the world's total economic activity (as measured by gross domestic product), and they control over 25% of the world's total assets. However, these corporations in aggregate employ less than 1% of the world's people.

- Large transnational corporations control 2/3 of all world trade.

- American corporations are actually experiencing decreasing taxes.

- Based on gross domestic product (what a given economy produces financially in goods and services), 52 of the world's wealthiest "nations" are not countries but rather corporations.

- American corporate CEOs are paid extremely high in comparison to top executives in most other countries. Additionally, American CEO compensation does not appear to correlate with job performance. CEO compensation recently rose 17%, while their corporations delivered lackluster profits, sinking stock prices, and even corporate failures and malfeasance.

- In most Latin American countries, 2% of the population owns 90% of the wealth.

- 22% of the world's total population earns less than $1 per day. 50% earn less than $2 per day.

- The world has 100 million people who live in what can be categorized as slums.

- In the cities of the developing world, 25% of the households live in poverty.

- 20% of the world population does not even have access to drinkable water. That equates to 1.2 billion people, or over 4 times the entire population of the United States.

It is in this domestic and global economic context that the American government recently passed legislation in 2003 granting fully 2/3 of a large tax break to the top 10% of American wage earners or alternatively, 58% of the tax break to the top 1% of wage earners.

This has brought the annual budget deficit (money America spends above what it brings in through taxation) to $455 billion, and it has required a raise in the maximum allowable debt ceiling (how much America can borrow) by an additional $1 trillion to $7.4 trillion. This amount of national debt is almost 4 times the tax revenues collected for an entire year.

Warren Buffet, a respected wealthy American capitalist and investor, analyzed this recent tax break legislation that was being presented to the American people as an "economic stimulus plan".

After studying the legislation's net effect on himself as compared to his receptionist, he wrote a scathing denunciation of the tax break legislation in the Washington Post. In it he wrote, "Supporters of making dividends tax-free like to paint critics as promoters of class warfare. The fact is, however, that their proposal promotes class *welfare*. For *my* class."

Shortly after the tax cut passed, the Pentagon proposed a reduction in military pay for troops, including national guard troops, serving overseas in Afghanistan and Iraq facing daily deaths. The pay reductions eliminate the paltry $75 per month in "imminent danger" compensation and $150 per month in "family separation allowances" for troops and their families already under severe financial pressure, many of them near poverty level.

Consumption in America and the World – It has been broadly estimated that the 4% of the world's population living in America consumes 40% to 50% of the world's resources. If a detailed analysis is conducted on energy resources alone, the following data is found.

Energy consumption for all countries in the world was 382 quadrillion Btu (382,000,000 billion British Thermal Units) in 1999. In 1999, America consumed 97 quadrillion Btu. Therefore, 4% of the world population living in America consumed 25% of the world energy. The closest energy consuming country was China with 21% of world population consuming 32 quadrillion Btu or 8% of world energy.

On Capitalism and Global Resources

Although there have been verifiable advancements in energy efficiency in America, on a per person basis people who live in the United States still consume twice as much energy as a person living in Europe or Japan. It is impossibly difficult to even meaningfully compare the typical energy consumption of an American to a person living in one of the developing or undeveloped countries.

The United States also has many more operating nuclear power reactors than any other country in the world; this despite the fact that many other nations depend much more on nuclear power to deliver the bulk of their electricity.

Pollution and Waste in America and the World - The United States is the largest emitter of pollutants, including carbon emissions. 4% of the world population living in America generates 25% of the world carbon emissions. This is due to many factors, a predominant one being the use of petroleum products to satisfy the country's immense transportation culture (for additional insight into this problem, see Oil Interests section). Also, in 1997 alone, America produced 110 million tons of solid waste.

Despite these facts, the United States government recently abandoned their support of the global environmental treaty, the Kyoto Protocol, citing that it would be too difficult for and unfair to American business. Additionally, other more domestic environmental protections, such as the Clean Air Act and the Clean Water Act, have been continually under attack and degraded by the current American government administration (see how this occurs in the Money and Democracy section).

Federal Tax Revenues – An unmistakable trend in the United States is a pronounced shift of the federal government tax revenue burden from corporations to individuals and families. This trend is occurring despite the fact that corporations were entities originally intended by America's founders to be granted a "privilege", and not a right, by the citizens to conduct business in its pursuit of profits. Corporations were not originally intended to have an innate right to operate freely and without cost in American society. The section on Corporate Personhood sheds more light on this topic.

The share of American tax revenue paid by corporations declined from 28% in 1956 to 12% in 1996. Corporate property taxes plunged from 45% in 1957 to 16% in 1995. One-third of America's largest corporations paid no taxes at all. And, if one is to look at all corporations doing business in America, fully a majority of them paid no (zero) taxes.

On the other hand, the family's share of American tax revenue rocketed from 17% in 1955 to 38% in 1998. Most recent data from 2001 indicates that tax revenues from corporations accounted for only 8% of the total, while tax revenues from individuals and families accounted for 53%.

In any given tax year, the remaining sources of federal tax revenue outside of corporate, individual, and family sources are employment (disability and unemployment), estate and gift, and excise tax revenues.

Oil Interests – (Much of the following information originated from and is discussed in great detail in "The Party's Over" by Richard Heinberg).

The earth is about 4.5 billion years old. For virtually all of human history (the most recent 500,000 years), the global population of humans has remained under ½ million people. It is only during the last 300 years that the world's population mushroomed to its present level of roughly 6 billion people.

It has been credibly argued that this very brief and relatively recent explosive growth in the world population of humans was due primarily to two important forces – the discovery of fossil fuels (coal, oil, and natural gas) as a dense useable source of energy and material for the production of other useful products, and the emergence of growing world markets undergoing rapid industrialization.

America is perhaps the best example of a country that has been the beneficiary of both of these defining forces, using the framework of capitalism as the organizing engine for its growth. By sheer chance, the formation and development of America as a country occurred during this same time period, the most recent 300 years.

America's lifestyle and economic growth is deeply dependent on the availability of fossil fuels such as oil, coal, and natural gas.

American daily life is littered with products that require petroleum. Not only is petroleum used to produce innumerable common products, but petroleum is also used to support America's immense agricultural food production and distribution system (e.g. fertilizers, pesticides, and equipment). It is not atypical for food products to travel 1,300 miles from the grower to consumer. And, of course, America's pervasive use of automobiles also increases the country's dependency on petroleum products.

The United States reached its peak of domestic oil production in the 1930s. Since that time, the America has always been strongly interested in available oil in other countries. Half of all American oil is imported. Two-thirds of the world's proven crude oil reserves are in the Middle East.

Even in peacetime, the American Pentagon is the world's biggest purchaser of refined oil products at 100 million barrels of petroleum per year, and this government agency accounts for fully 80% of all federal government energy use. This does not include the vast amounts of additional petroleum products that the military consumes when they actually execute an overseas military campaign such as the Persian Gulf War or the Iraq War. Therefore, the American military itself has powerful interests in securing petroleum resources for its own survival and its own consumption.

Alarmingly, given this present state of affairs, it has been credibly asserted that America, and more broadly the world, will soon suffer a global oil depletion crisis severely impacting both modern lifestyle and economic growth.

If this assertion is accepted, one is confronted with a clear implied choice for America: Either fight in more wars to secure access to an increasingly elusive and depleted petroleum resource and potentially damage the planet. Or, create and promote less petroleum-dependent lifestyles, and invest heavily into conservation and renewable energy technologies (a non-exhaustible and typically environmentally cleaner resource) to secure a longer-term sustainable future for America and the rest of the world.

Most Americans are unaware that the American military spent from $100 billion to more than $1 trillion, between the years 1980 and 1993, in order to protect American interests in the Middle East region alone. Additionally, American governments and multinational oil corporations have tended to support and foster dictatorships in the foreign countries in which they operate to keep their oil resources secure.

This is one of the reasons why the American government has frequently supported brutal tyrannical regimes overseas. The intention of this support has been to provide security for American oil company investments overseas, often at the expense of natives agitating for freedom and improved lives in their own countries.

It should also be observed that as much as American's lament high and rising gasoline prices at the gas pump, retail gasoline prices in America are typically 1/2 to 1/3 the price for gasoline in most countries of Europe and Asia.

America's Crisis of Confidence – It has become common for American citizens, when speaking honestly and frankly, to express a definite loss of confidence in both the American government and its big business sector.

American citizens clearly understand that their country possesses a generously funded military program with a massive inventory of high technology airplanes, ships, submarines, tanks and other war equipment. For some American citizens this is, in and of itself, a source of national pride.

However, on a deeper level, most Americans also understand what President Dwight Eisenhower meant when he said, "Every gun that is made, every warship launched, every rocket fired, signifies in a final sense a theft from those who are hungry and are not fed, those who are cold and not clothed. The world in arms is not spending money alone. It is spending the sweat of its laborers, the genius of its scientists, the hopes of its children."

To make matters worse, American citizens have for years felt increasingly disconnected from and largely irrelevant to domestic politics (for added perspective on this topic, please see the Money and Democracy section). It has even been feared by some citizens that as the common people become more disconnected from political life, that America will move toward a fascist-like government.

The loss of confidence has not been confined to the government, but now also extends to the private sector. This is with good reason. In 2001 and 2002 alone, 77 large companies from a broad variety of economic sectors and industries filed for bankruptcy. The result has been the failure of many very large American corporations with its attendant loss of jobs, and the destruction of the savings of millions of Americans.

The list of large business failures and resulting lawsuits, many due to corruption and illegal, unethical, or immoral business practices, is too long to cite here. Some of the notable examples are Enron, Arthur Anderson, WorldCom, Tyco, Imclone, Montana Power, Global Crossing, Adelphia, and most of the major investment banks.

The government, through the Securities Exchange Commission and Justice Department, appears unable or unwilling to adequately control and penalize offending executives and to substantively address real problems within the various industries. Legal experts now concede that top executives, for example those at failed Enron and WorldCom, may never face prosecution. These business failures alone wiped out 35,000 jobs and destroyed upwards of $1 billion in employee pensions.

Ironically, large corporations have even more immunity from being punished for illegal or unethical behavior (for more on this perspective, see the Corporate Personhood section). An example is a recent United States federal judge ruling that levied a "moderate" settlement of $750 million against WorldCom/MCI for its $11 billion accounting scandal which destroyed approximately $200 billion in shareholder wealth. The judge and the Securities Exchange Commission did not want to punish the corporation so much as to cause the death of a large corporation affecting the employment prospects of the company's remaining 50,000 employees. This settlement effectively eliminated any future prospects to recover investment money for shareholders.

This is the same corporation that received upwards of $772 million in contracts from the American government in 2002, and despite their fraudulent accounting recently received new military contract work as part of a $45 million communications rebuilding project related to the Iraq War.

And now, facing increased widespread joblessness the American public has also become more vulnerable to malfeasance by corporate executives because the general public now owns more shares of company stock either directly or indirectly through their pensions, 401K, IRA, and mutual fund holdings.

Another recent example is the close relationship between ex-Enron top executives and the President George W. Bush administration, and the non-publicly disclosed correspondence and activities relating to the development of America's national energy policy behind closed-doors at the White House's Energy Policy Board.

Credible concerns have been raised that national energy policy has been excessively influenced by industry heavyweights such as Enron and many other corporate players.

The collapse of Enron resulted in a $50 billion loss to pension and mutual fund investors alone, and resolution of Enron's finances will likely pay its creditors less than 1/5 of the $67 billion owed. The United States Security and Exchange commission levied a fine on Enron's investment bankers (Citigroup and J.P. Morgan Chase) of only $300 million for their role in Enron's escapades. This amounts to roughly one week's profit to the banks. Furthermore, under a new provision of the recent Sarbanes-Oxley law, a portion of the fine will be credited against any liability levied on the banks through private civil securities litigation. Finally, no jail time was pursued for the responsible investment banking executives.

Too frequently, the relationships between these large corporations and the American government are much too close for comfort.

Corporate Personhood – (Much of the information in this section is discussed in great detail in "Unequal Protection" by Thom Hartmann).

When discussing America's private sector, it is useful to distinguish between big business (the small group of large multinational corporations) and small business (the vast majority of businesses). Most people concerned with the conduct of commercial activities are far more often concerned with the powers and actions of big businesses, and not as concerned with small businesses. This is for good reason. These two categories of private industry are two very different animals.

On Capitalism and Global Resources

Big businesses are typically characterized by very large multiple revenue and cash flow streams, extensive domestic market reach, access to raw materials and labor in foreign markets, and sales into multiple foreign markets. They often powerfully influence global policies that have geographically far-reaching implications, and they typically organize their global material and capital flows in a manner to minimize taxes and maximize profits to their shareholders.

Generally, big businesses are much less connected to the local communities that they serve, as compared to small businesses. And, typically big businesses have ready access to large sums of money and teams of expensive lawyers. These resources can be used to highly influence government legislation and regulations that are intended to ensure that the interests of "the people" are protected and that commercial activities are adequately moderated.

This is not to imply that big business and all people who work in them are inherently bad people. Of course, the vast majority of workers in large corporations are also simply trying to earn an honest living, be good citizens, and become good people. It is simply to acknowledge the global reach of large multinational corporations, and their inordinately powerful leverage because of their very nature.

This is also not to imply that the only manner in which a corporate management can choose to behave is in the single-minded pursuit of profit maximization. It is, however, to recognize that in the real world it is all too common and easy for corporate behavior to be highly if not dominantly skewed toward profit maximization.

This issue relating to large corporations and the people's attempts to control and constrain potentially

111

damaging corporate activities is old. In America, it dates back to the country's earliest founding years.

American colonists were keenly aware of the overreaching powers of large multinational corporations. In fact, it is not commonly known that a primary motivation for the colonist's demand for independence from England was to get out from under the thumb of one of the largest multinational corporations of its time, the East India Company. The East India Company was a large British corporation established by Queen Elizabeth specifically to compete with the Dutch in the lucrative global spice market. England wanted to monopolize or at least dominate this lucrative sector of world trade, and it established the East India Company to do so.

This is the same corporation that owned the *Mayflower*, the ship that delivered early American pilgrims. This is the same corporation that adopted a company flag design upon which (perhaps fittingly) the American flag was modeled by the colonists and produced by Betsy Ross. And, this is the same corporation that established a private military and police force so that it could advance its own business interests.

Through "gunboat diplomacy", the British and the East India Company eventually came to dominate commerce in India, to force the trading of opium into China, and to dominate international trade into the new American colonies.

However, early American colonists wanted to import and export products without having to work through the British government or the East India Company. And so, many of them set up small entrepreneurial operations to do so much to the consternation of the British.

Becoming arguably the first American example of corporate lobbying for market power, the East India

Company lobbied the British government for legislation and regulation intended to destroy the American small business competitors, and to help establish trade monopolies in their favor. Examples of British laws that were created as a direct result of this corporate lobbying effort are "An Act For the Restraining and Punishing Privateers & Pirates", the Townshend Acts of 1767, and the Tea Act of 1773.

The expanding American colonies were becoming a huge market for tea and many resident colonists wanted the option to buy less expensive tea from the Dutch, or to secure other alternative sources of tea for greater variety and lower price. This was a real economic threat to the interests of the British government and the East India Company.

Unknown to many Americans, the Tea Act was designed to establish a tea trade monopoly for the East India Company, to exempt the company from paying government taxes, and to even award the company a tax refund on tea that the company could not sell. This is no different than the numerous examples of present day corporate lobbying and "corporate subsidies" in America. For an expanded perspective, see the Money and Democracy section and the Corporate Subsidies and Supports section.

The East India Company, with complicity and support from the British government, relentlessly strived to drive American small companies out of business by dumping cheap untaxed tea into the American colonies.

The end result was that a ragtag group of armed American colonists disguised as American Indians, strode down to a Boston wharf where three East India Company ships were berthed in the harbor. The colonists boarded the ships, and proceeded to throw 342 opened crates of tea into the harbor.

Even after the American colonists won their independence from Britain, the East India Company continued to persist in its efforts to dominate American commerce. This factor helped to start the War of 1812.

Therefore, the Boston Tea Party was arguably the first large-scale American protest against conditions resulting from the predatory and oppressive actions of large multinational corporations, and the governments that protect them. Resisting corporate and government power is as American as apple pie. In fact, early American governments including those under Thomas Jefferson, James Madison, and Andrew Jackson openly worried about constraining the power of large multinational corporate interests in order to protect the resources and power of the people.

One corporation, the Second Bank of the United States, was eventually put out of business by early American government for trying too aggressively to extend its influence into the houses of government. History therefore teaches that it is not impossible for governments to resist becoming puppets of large corporate interests, and in fact this was the prevailing sentiment for many early American political leaders.

The first 10 American Bill of Rights were designed specifically to award important powers and rights to common people, and not to institutions like governments, religious organizations, commercial monopolies, wealthy individuals, or powerful corporations. Thomas Jefferson himself argued for a Constitutional amendment that would prevent companies from growing to a point that they would dominate industries or gain the power to influence American government (Oh, how far we have wandered, Mr. Jefferson).

For decades, American government at all levels (national, state, and local) frequently and commonly passed laws that were deliberately and openly designed to protect people from the adverse affects of large corporate predatory power. Corporate power was a well-understood reality to early Americans and their elected officials; it was not a theoretical hypothetical abstract notion.

However, beginning in the 1870s powerful railroad companies and their owners began a legal assault on the government because it wanted to relax the constraints levied on them. Up to that point in American history, corporations had always been considered "artificial legal entities", and therefore subordinate to the government, which was itself subordinate to the people. During this time period, the railroad companies also began the practice of hiring ex-legislators or ex-government personnel as their lawyers (a practice which continues to this day).

Ironically, it was an ex-Illinois legislator by the name of Abraham Lincoln who became one of the earliest lawyers to represent the railroad companies. He joined the legal efforts of the railroad companies after trying unsuccessfully to secure a job arguing for the government against the railroad companies.

In his arguments for the Illinois Central Railroad, he based his legal position on a theory that corporations should be considered a "person" with regards to taxation rights and protections. Lincoln was unsuccessful in securing the "corporate personhood" designation for the railroad, but he was successful in securing important accommodations with respect to the disputed tax. (As a side note, the railroad company subsequently refused to pay Lincoln's legal bill, and Lincoln ultimately had to sue the company to receive his wages).

Throughout his presidency, however, Lincoln grew increasingly disturbed by the growing power of large corporations such as the railroad companies. Corporate interests seemed to infiltrate all levels of government in order to secure their market monopolies. The results were huge profits for large American corporations. Through their influence on government, corporations also got laws passed specifically designed to permit the immigration of cheap foreign labor with the intended effect to break labor strikes and to reduce the wages of common laborers in America.

Corruption between corporations and the American government continued to grow out of control. The powerful railroad companies continued to receive free land grants and millions of dollars in other tax abatements and subsidies, ostensibly to encourage them to extend their railroad lines.

The wealthy railroad companies continued to make the "corporate personhood" argument in United States courts no matter how many times they were rejected. However, because the railroad corporations could afford an unrelenting and sustained lobbying effort in the halls of government (unlike what most common American citizens could do), they kept their case alive until they finally received the legal break they were seeking. Their chance came in 1886.

In that year, a Supreme Court decision was returned concerning the case of *Santa Clara County versus Southern Pacific Railroad Company*. Santa Clara County in California had sued Southern Pacific Railroad for unpaid taxes. The railroad's lawyers included in their arguments the suggestion that corporations (artificial persons) should have the same rights as individuals (natural persons) as granted under the 14th Amendment to the Constitution (which was intended to grant rights to freed slaves).

The court did not rule on this 14th Amendment argument, but a court reporter included mention of a verbal discussion that had occurred between the judge and lawyers regarding the argument. Notes based on this dialog made its way into a legal headnote in a case record book. A legal headnote is a comment note having no legal weight.

This entry subsequently led people to the erroneous belief that one outcome of the case was that the railroad corporation was considered a person protected by the provisions in the 14th Amendment. The ultimate end result over time has been that the American legal establishment has improperly validated corporate claim to rights originally intended only for human American citizens under the 14th Amendment.

These rights were numerous and included free speech (allowing corporations to kill laws that would prevent them from lobbying or giving money to politicians), the right of privacy (allowing corporations to prevent forced disclosure of records and site inspections), and protections against discrimination (allowing corporations to block local governments desire to tax chain stores at a higher rate than local businesses).

Ironically, at the same time that hundreds of corporations were being awarded rights originally created and intended for applications to human beings, women and non-white human beings continued to be denied basic rights of citizenship such as the right to vote. Therefore, American courts had validated corporations as "citizens", before they even validated real human beings living within the borders of America as "citizens".

It is in this climate that certain state governments became particularly pro-business and even modified their individual state constitutions and passed other laws to make their state more "business friendly". This is why so many American corporations, located throughout the country, identify Delaware and New Jersey as their states of incorporation.

As large multicultural corporations have grown even more immense and more global in its reach, countries throughout the world (particularly the poorer countries) have been forced to pass their own laws and regulations, or even modify their national constitutions to attract the investment of wealthy corporations in the hopes of bringing desperately needed jobs to their people. Unfortunately for many countries, this reward has come at a terrible price (see the following Corporate Subsidies and Supports section).

Corporate Subsidies and Supports – America operates within an economic system that frequently and openly subsidizes large corporations with large amounts of public money. There are many examples.

One example is the numerous financial bailouts with public money when large businesses fail, such as the Savings and Loan failure. There is, in fact, a recurring historical pattern of using American taxpayer money to cover for big business failures. Looking at recent history alone, this type of public bailout has occurred in 1987, 1989, and in 1991.

A second example of public subsidies to large corporations is the availability of large amounts of taxpayer money to conduct early technology research and development. Technology originating from this work is often subsequently transferred to private corporations (in the form of protected intellectual property) so that they may commercialize the technology and earn corporate profits.

Some prominent industries that have benefited immensely from this use of public investment money include the telecommunications, aircraft, and electronics industries. In fact, the American Pentagon and military establishment (1.5 million employees/soldiers) and its defense contractors are prototypes of large organizational institutions that owe their very existence to public subsidies of taxpayer money.

A third example of a subsidy that governments increasingly give to large multinational corporations are those that are offered to corporations if they decide to locate a new facility in their geographic area. This is true both domestically and internationally. Luring big employers is a common method for local politicians to boost their own reelection prospects by bringing desperately needed jobs to a region. Unfortunately, it is increasingly common that they must concede to pay an extortive price to lure the new tenants.

Examples of this third type of subsidy are Daimler-Benz's selection to build a new factory in Alabama (with hundreds of millions in tax benefits, virtually free land, and the use of tax payer money to build supporting infrastructure), and the many instances involving poorer countries such as Mexico or the Czech Republic bidding for hosting rights for rich American factories.

Particularly when the local community has little or no negotiating power as compared to the large multinational corporation, it is not uncommon for a small minority of people in the community to benefit from the corporate investment, while the lifestyle of the majority is driven down. In this case, local residents essentially pay for much of the facility, and if not shielded by labor protections they end up working for alarmingly low wages and little to no benefits, and sometimes they must even eventually pay for environmental cleanup.

Conceptually, these examples suggest a notion whereby "profits are privatized, and costs are socialized". In other words, big corporations generate profits for private sector investors, while the very real costs associated with the facility (such as infrastructure degradation, pollution, disposal of toxic waste, etc.) become the broader responsibility of the common community taxpayer.

And the litany continues. In July 2003, the Ways and Means Committee in the United States Congress announced a new proposal to reduce the corporate tax rate by 3 percent. This corporate tax relief is intended to offset an existing annual $5 billion corporate tax break that Congress must eliminate because of threatened action by the International Trade Court. Fewer than 200 of the largest corporations will reap 90% of the new tax break benefit. The Ways and Means Committee Chairman has the backing of some of America's largest multinational corporations.

These are all examples of real government corporate subsidy spending that, rightly or wrongly, have the ultimate effect of reducing the pot of money available to fund the many other legitimate American societal needs. Interestingly, however, most Americans have difficulty perceiving these actions as corporate "welfare or subsidies". They are often viewed as "reform, economic support, and protection of American jobs" while subsidies to real human beings are typically portrayed and viewed as "waste, welfare, and giveaways".

The Lost Commons – The concept of "the commons" is an old one with respect to American colonial usage. The commons was literally a piece of land that was subject to common use. An example would be the grazing ground that all townspeople would use for their animals. Over time, the notion of the commons has been expanded to include all those resources owned and utilized by all people (the masses) for common benefit.

This concept also has early roots in American history, as Benjamin Franklin himself was a big supporter and promoter of institutions and projects that would benefit broadly all American citizens. Resources or services considered in the commons are typically essential and necessary resources, and not luxuries.

They are resources essential to daily life such as clean water, clean air, energy, electricity, and telecommunications (and arguably even education and healthcare). However, they may also include resources that historically have been (for good reason) considered owned by the public and licensed to private industry, such as the public broadcast airways.

Historically, the American government has also imposed government constraint and regulation, for various reasons, on important large industries such as the airlines, banking, and media (television, radio, newspapers, magazines).

In recent history, the American government has embarked on an aggressive crusade to deregulate and privatize many of these industries under the presumption that deregulation and privatization would lead to higher efficiency, less waste, lower prices, and superior service. This presumption is grounded in the belief that Darwinian competitive pressures experienced by private sector companies can be usefully applied to improve the performance of organizations responsible for the production and distribution of resources from the commons, or improve the markets of other industries historically subjected to government regulation.

In general, industry deregulation has been an issue almost solely promoted and advanced by industry players on behalf of their own corporate interests, and did not originate from the common American people. Many of the early results have been devastating.

Down the line, deregulation of critically important industries has led to disastrous results. Examples include recent unethical behavior by companies in the investment banking industry, and the spectacular failure of large corporations due to illegal and unethical behavior and greed. Case examples might include Enron, Arthur Anderson, Montana Power, WorldCom, Tyco, Adelphia, and Global Crossing.

And within this disastrous deregulated environment, there are many people who bounce back and forth in their careers between working within a government agency (which is tasked with protecting common resources on behalf of all American citizens) and working within private industry (which has its own business agenda concerning government oversight of their industries). This has resulted in massive conflict-of-interest, or at the very least, the appearance of conflict-of-interest.

An example is the United States Department of the Interior, which is tasked with protecting public lands and national parks. The department has arguably become a revolving door of senior government administrators and senior executives of private companies with business before the agency. The result has become a case of the "fox guarding the henhouse" as private industry exerts its influence inside the corridors of government to pave the way for industry exploitation of common lands.

The current United States administration has already issued an executive order to the Bureau of Land Management, an agency within the Department of the Interior, to remove or weaken obstacles that slow the development of oil and gas in key regions in America. Many of these provisional obstacles were designed intentionally to protect the environment of the common public lands. This particular executive order directly impacts several areas in the Western United States including Montana, Wyoming, Utah, Colorado, and New Mexico.

This problem of the "revolving door" between senior government administrators and senior executives in private industry, and the conflict-of-interest that naturally occurs is not unusual. Other government departments such as the Department of Defense have experienced the same problem.

The trend toward privatization has also affected the American military where private companies are increasingly providing military-oriented services including strategic planning, logistics, facilities construction, technology operations, maintenance, and even deployment of mercenary combat troops.

This is a global, essentially completely unregulated industry. The companies are essentially a "military force for hire". It is also not comforting that some of the companies have also been involved in dubious and controversial activities, even non-military related activities. There are a number of these global military services companies in existence, including Kellogg, Brown and Root, a subsidiary of Halliburton (ex-CEO is the United States Vice President).

This trend toward privatization and deregulation has been extended globally as the American government and multinational corporations, along with international agencies such as the World Bank and the International Monetary Fund, exert immense pressure on developing and undeveloped countries for political and economic reform. The desired end is often to pry open their local markets so that vastly stronger American competition may enter to do business, and to open up their commons resources to American ownership and exploitation. These actions are often demanded even before developing countries are strong enough themselves to manage this type of change and to compete adequately with new American corporate competitors.

In a real sense, the American government and its powerful multinational corporations are prying open weaker and more vulnerable countries of the world essentially for the enrichment of American corporations, while frequently causing huge harm to the weaker country's environment, people, national independence and sovereignty.

Symptomatic of American capitalism out of control globally is the example of Philip Morris, a large multinational American corporation. The company was recently deeply embarrassed regarding marketing activities of its tobacco products in the poor emerging Czech Republic. The American corporation funded a report to the Czech Republic asserting that tobacco use by its citizens would result in health care, pension, and housing cost savings because of the early mortality of people due to smoking.

International Trade – It is not uncommon for America to use its large domestic markets, its influence at the World Trade Organization and United Nations, and its investment dollars (either directly or indirectly through international finance institutions) as powerful trade negotiating weapons that often force or coerce poorer nations into submitting to harsh demands.

Examples include the use of international trade embargos (preventing trade) or trade sanctions (trade penalties). In essence, America can restrict or eliminate the ability of a target country to trade internationally in order to cripple or destabilize the target country's economy, and thus its government. These actions essentially destroy the foreign country's ability to bring wealth into their own country through trade, and disrupts the lives of its common citizens by making products for daily needs unavailable. Recent examples would include America's trade policies with respect to Iraq and Cuba.

Not commonly known is that the recent explosive growth in international trade is not really as it appears. Approximately 50% of what is counted by the federal government as international trade are really transactions within large multinational companies that are simply moving product and material across borders to manufacture at lower costs, to sell at higher prices, and to minimize their taxes and maximize company profits.

One example of this type of activity is the cross-border movement of product between the United States and Mexican Maquiladoras (low-cost, customs-free manufacturing operations). This arrangement is designed to allow American products to be produced at lower costs while shifting industrial environmental impact from America to Mexico. Unfortunately, even Mexico now faces losing investment and manufacturing to other poorer countries as large multinational corporations continue to rush to the lowest wage countries to protect their profits and remain globally competitive.

True international trade (which either brings wealth into America, or moves wealth into the economies of other nations), however, has not grown as much. In other words, the wealth is primarily circulating within the large multinational companies.

Recently, Central American leaders met to discuss and debate a possible CAFTA (Central American Free Trade Agreement) with the American government. After studying the proposal, and considering the now verifiable effects of NAFTA on Mexico's state-of-affairs, the leaders concluded that accepting a CAFTA agreement with America would be harmful to the Central American countries.

It is believed by many people that CAFTA would result in the exploitation of poor Central American workers, failure to protect the local environment, raiding of critical national utilities and resources (such as electricity, water, and energy) by American private industry, and a risk of total destruction of agricultural farmers by exposing them to the overwhelming power of large American multinational companies. Central American leaders are fearful that they will be forced to accept this trade agreement because of the political and economic pressure exerted by the American government.

Immigrant Labor – Besides Native Americans, America's population is composed entirely of ex-slaves and foreign immigrants and their descendents. While the earliest years brought immigrants from primarily Europe, recent years have brought immigrants from a much more diverse number of countries, including many from non-European regions such as Latin America and Asia. Outside of Native Americans, America's *entire* labor force is essentially immigrant labor.

Immigrant contributions to America abound. These include the reclamation of land and cultivation of agricultural products, the building of the transcontinental railway, the fishing, poultry and meat production industry, the construction industry, the manufactured and assembled goods industries, and domestic housekeeping and gardening.

Illegal immigration is the unlawful presence of a person from outside of the United States. This may occur through a variety of situations including a person that crosses a national border unlawfully, a person that overstays a limited-time work or education visa, and a person that falsifies immigration documents to gain entry. The practice of illegally immigrating to America is pervasive throughout American history, and it has been done by virtually all racial groups.

Nevertheless, illegal or recent immigrants have been a common and recurrent target or scapegoat for American citizens to blame for a wide range of problems. The denouncing of illegal or recent immigrants is particularly vehement during times of economic depression or tight labor markets.

Ironically, this national ambivalence and even animosity toward both legal and illegal recent immigrants has occurred despite the fact that America has grown and prospered through the work of its many immigrants. American citizens enjoy low prices for goods and services and a very high standard of living largely due to immigrant laborers who are willing to work very hard for low wages and little job security. Historically, large

American corporations have even actively recruited sources of cheap foreign labor to produce goods or services, to boost profits, or even to break up labor strikes.

Recently, many immigrants to America have been from Mexico. As an example of how American capitalistic interests can become linked to immigration policy, the American government is conditioning future Mexican immigration policy on the privatization of Mexico's oil industry. This action is designed to pressure the Mexican government into allowing American corporations to invest into Mexico's oil production resources, thus increasing American corporate ownership and control of yet another global oil resource. Only then will certain levels of Mexican immigration be allowed into America.

This view toward immigration stands in stark contrast to the sentiment espoused in Emma Lazarus's poem for the Statue of Liberty, "Give me your tired, your poor, Your huddled masses yearning to breathe free". Today, she might add, "… if you give me a cut of your oil."

World Trade Organization (WTO) – This is the international institution that establishes international trade rules. Its predecessor was the General Agreement on Tariffs and Trade (GATT). The United States is an active member of the 145-nation member organization that issues rules applying to over 90% of international trade.

Because WTO policy requires approval by member countries, the organization moves relatively slowly. However, WTO power is considerable since the organization can issue international trade sanctions. There is current controversy with the WTO institution because its actions are believed to be highly influenced by wealthy corporate interests and the institution's deliberations and decisions lack transparency (are not disclosed to the public).

If the United States government has difficulty getting what it wants through the WTO, they will often craft bilateral (country-to-country) or multilateral (multiple countries) trade agreements, while exerting demands on those countries in order to win American government approval for the trade agreement.

Examples of these American trade agreements are NAFTA and CAFTA (see International Trade section). Countries, particularly poor countries, find the prospect of trade access to the large and rich American market so appealing that they often agree to harsh American demands that ultimately hurt their own domestic economy (a very common example is opening up agricultural markets to products from rich American corporations, to the detriment of native farmers and growers).

Obviously, the WTO is an organization that wields important influence over international trade, and is an important institution to countries at all stages of economic development. Undeveloped or developing countries are particularly vulnerable and must frequently agree to domestic trade and treasury policies that are preferred by powerful industrialized countries such as America, in order to win acceptance to join the WTO. Once a country is a member of the WTO, it becomes involved in negotiations with respect to international trade disputes of global importance.

A recent example is the controversy surrounding the trading of genetically modified (GM) foods. Genetically modified foods are already distributed and consumed pervasively in the United States with no special labeling requirement (It might be an interesting exercise to study why and how this happened in America). Many citizens of European countries, and even other non-European countries, object to consuming GM foods without at least some type of labeling on the food product that tells the consumer that the food is genetically modified.

The American government has viewed this largely European position as an unfair trade impediment. There is controversy regarding the ultimate health risks of GM foods, much like there has been controversy regarding the long-term safety and risks of nuclear power. However, as demonstrated by the rocky history of nuclear power in America, free people are reluctant to give up the right to make personal choices (especially when it concerns their health), regardless of what science indicates about the risks. Personal choice is fundamental and an important aspect of American freedom. In the future, the conflicts regarding GM products will be played out in part at the WTO.

America will often coordinate its foreign policy and trade policy, with its powerful influence at internationally oriented institutions such as the WTO, IMF (see following sections), World Bank, Ex-Im, OPIC, and the United Nations.

International Monetary Fund (IMF) and United Nations World Bank – These are international lending institutions with money supplied primarily by wealthy industrialized countries. The decisions made by these institutions can be and have been used to reward or punish poorer countries. American influence at these institutions is also often used in conjunction with trade agreements or international trade sanctions or embargoes when America negotiates with other countries.

Agreements from these institutions often require American-favored behaviors by poor countries in order to secure investment money. These commonly include wide-scale privatization of industries (as opposed to publicly-owned), curtailment of regulations (allowing freer action by foreign private companies), the elimination or reduction of state money directed toward social good (such as social safety nets or medical care), and changes to their internal treasury and trade policies (such as money supply, currency controls, tariffs, and government expenditures).

It has been argued that the net effect of these coerced actions is to transform poor but formerly sovereign and economically independent countries into profitable multinational corporation labor or consumer markets. Under proper economic and political conditions, wealth can be more efficiently transferred from poorer nations to the United States. As an end result, the poor country gets even more poor and highly dependent on continuing aid from the wealthy industrialized nations.

United States Export-Import Bank (Ex-Im) and Overseas Private Investment Corporation (OPIC) – These are American government agencies, funded by American taxpayer money, and located within the Department of Commerce. These institutions lend money for large, capital-intensive international projects, often with mandatory provisions for foreign countries to purchase American goods and services. Ex-Im and OPIC are commonly used to finance commercial projects overseas with an eye toward boosting American exports, which transfers more wealth from other nations into the United States.

An example of Ex-Im involvement with an American corporation concerns Enron, the now-defunct and scandalized American energy-trading corporation. Enron received $3.6 billion for its international infrastructure projects through the Ex-Im, OPIC, and allied agencies. The United Nations World Bank gave approximately the same amount of capital to Enron. This is again essentially American taxpayer money subsidizing Enron projects.

Enron's moves into the international energy markets could be characterized in the following manner: Go to a poor country, offer to build critically needed energy infrastructure at a high price, and do the construction work with money provided by American taxpayers (through the Ex-Im, OPIC, and the World Bank). In addition, force the poor country to assume much of the project risks by mandating that they invest substantially into the project. Operate the facility, and repatriate (bring back) the profits from the overseas operation to Enron coffers in the United States.

Electronic International Financial Transactions - In recent years, there has been an explosion in the movement of money between countries. Capital now flows between countries in vastly higher volumes, and much more rapidly and freely than ever before.

Money is transferred between countries for a variety of reasons. For example, money can be transferred to pay for imported goods or services, or for long-term investments. Or, money can be transferred for financial speculation (e.g. to bet on short-term changes in foreign currency).

It is revealing to compare the composition of international financial transactions that occurred from the late 19th century through 1980, with recent transactions during the 1990s. Before the 1990s, 90% of international financial transactions involved transfers of money to pay for goods or services, or for long-term international investments. By the 1990s, the statistics were reversed. Only 5% were transfers of this type, and 95% of financial transactions involved money transferred between countries for financial speculation purposes.

Furthermore, the transfers of money occur primarily between the 3 large global economic regions of the United States, Europe, and Japan. This is analogous to an immense global gambling casino in which the game is dominated by relatively few rich gamblers who are betting on their own economic future as well as the future of other economies throughout the world.

On International Aggression

Chapter Summary – Contrary to a belief held by many Americans that the United States acts through violence or force reluctantly, and generally only under conditions of clear national defense (such as when America entered World War II after the Japanese attack on Pearl Harbor), America has a recurring history of international aggression. America does not maintain military bases in 100 countries without reason.

Some important historical events have been publicized and thus are well known by most American citizens. However, many events were either covert (secret) or they were dismally underreported by the American media. These events are not as well known.

A common and recurring practice for the American government is to demonize and vilify foreign leaders as a precondition prior to launching an international invasion. Ironically, in too many cases these same foreign leaders rose to power and oppressed their own national populations with the ardent support of the same American government that now vilifies them.

In fact, if viewed objectively it can be credibly argued that through much of its history, America has behaved in a manner indicative of being one of the world's most active international aggressors. It can also be credibly asserted that while this has occurred, its citizenry has been largely unaware, isolated, and unaffected by these international events.

Recently, to the surprise of many even in its own government, the United States administration has embarked on the implementation of a global geopolitical plan based largely on the fundamental belief that violence perpetrated globally is acceptable to promote the spread of democracy and to solidify American global power. This plan is being promoted somewhat as a new American "manifest destiny" (for historical context of this term, see American Indians section).

One articulation of the philosophy is found in a report issued in 2000 by the Project for the New American Century, an American global leadership think tank.

The document, *Rebuilding America's Defenses*, asserts that because America now stands alone as the only global military superpower post-Cold War, that America should take advantage of the situation by boosting its already high level of military expenditures and aggressively imposing its global vision and will (ostensibly to bring peace, freedom, democracy and liberation to other people) across international boundaries and throughout the world. Furthermore, in support of this higher mission, America would be called upon to finance and engage in multiple simultaneous international wars.

On a global level, the intent of the plan is to proliferate even further America's military presence to more locations throughout the world, at times relying on a more mobile force. One objective of the plan is to establish a *permanent* American security presence in the Middle East. The document also indicates that the American government should feel threatened by China's growth and development. In response, it is suggested that America also establish a *permanent* military presence in Southeast Asia.

The report asserts that because it is impossible to completely halt the spread of weapons-of-mass-destruction technology throughout the world, the United States must abandon weapons control as a defense strategy and commit to building more varieties of and even more powerful nuclear weapons. Finally, the report also identifies outer space as the next frontier for American control. In fact, the document actually uses the terms "control the new international commons".

Some experts have observed that a rough articulation of the plan is expressed as: America intends to rule the world (as opposed to being simply one member of the international global community), that it intends to perpetually remain the ruler, and that America reserves the right to attack any form of opposition resisting this aim. (See www.newamericancentury.org. There is a Statement of Principles, and the report is downloadable from that website. This information was developed largely by senior American government officials, military personnel, and military industry insiders. You will recognize some of the names.)

Current American political and military doctrine also generally asserts that direct conflict should be avoided with strong countries, and war should be waged only with weak countries. And, when America does attack a weaker country, it must win rapidly and decisively to serve as a clear demonstration of American military power, and to avoid inevitable dissention to war over time by American citizens and the broader international community.

How does war between nations begin, why do nations invade other nations, and why do seemingly intelligent citizens of countries often enthusiastically jump on the war and patriotism bandwagon – like what happened in Germany during the 1930s and 1940s?

The answer might lie in comments made by Nazi war criminal Hermann Goering at the Nuremberg Trials in 1946, after the end of World War II. He said,

"Naturally, the common people don't want war...but, after all, it is the leaders of the country who determine the policy and it is always a simple matter to drag the people along, whether it is a democracy or a fascist dictatorship or a Parliament or a Communist dictatorship... Voice or no voice, the people can always be brought to the bidding of the leaders. That is easy. All you have to do is tell them they are being attacked and denounce the pacifists for lack of patriotism and exposing the country to danger. It works the same way in any country."

Unfortunately, through words and by deeds, the American government has confirmed to the world community that the future will likely include increased international aggression by America.

It is, however, important to understand that this behavior has deep roots in American history. This section may also give the reader some tangible indication as to the answer to the infamous national question, "Why do they Hate Us?"

Mexico – In 1846, 43 years after Thomas Jefferson doubled the size of the United States through the Louisiana Purchase from France, President James Polk had his eye on taking California from the nation of Mexico.

The American government provoked an attack from Mexico in April of that year as it moved into the Mexican territories, a mere 25 years after the Mexican people had finally won its independence from Spain. Through prosecution of this war, the United States took about ½ of Mexico's territories including land that are now the states of California, New Mexico, Texas, Nevada, Utah, Arizona, and part of Colorado.

Thousands of people were killed in the battles, and many of the victims were civilian women and children. Tragically, when American soldiers returned home from the war flush with land warrants awarded by the United States government, greedy speculators bought up the warrants at fire sale prices from soldiers who were desperate for cash. It is known that many large fortunes were made by speculators preying on American soldiers returning from the War with Mexico.

Ironically, after the war the American government paid Mexico a token $15 million and an American newspaper declared, "We take nothing by conquest ... Thank God"

Cuba - America invaded Cuba in 1898 as a part of the Spanish American War, and the United States government issued a congressional declaration renouncing any desire "to exercise sovereignty, jurisdiction, or control" over Cuba. However, when the war ended, the American government, as was similarly done at the end of the Iraq War, appointed a government in Cuba headed by an American General.

Before eventually returning the government back to Cuban rule in 1902, the United States government forced Cuba to open its markets and industries to American business, to grant America the rights to a military base, and to grant the right to intervene in Cuban affairs - which the United States government did 4 times between 1906 and 1920.

In 1912, after the American occupation formally ended, the white-dominated Cuban government massacred more than 6,000 black Cubans. Many of these black Cubans were not only veterans of the Spanish American War, but they had also organized a black political party to fight for racial equality. United States troops protected American business interests and citizens, but did nothing to interfere with the massacre.

During the 1950s, a Cuban leader by the name of Fidel Castro led a successful popular uprising for liberation against an American endorsed leader, Fulgencio Batista. Under the Batista regime, 95% of Cuba's wealth was controlled by a small group of American business interests and Cuban elite.

From the earliest beginnings of the Castro regime, the American government has continually attempted to destabilize the Cuban government through covert military operations, direct and indirect attacks, assassination attempts, terrorism, trade embargoes, destruction of food crops, and support of dissidents. 10 million Cubans have died, in large part through the effects of these actions and policies.

Ironically, in an apparent replay with regards to history, the United States President when commenting on the American invasion of Iraq stated, "We have no ambition in Iraq, except to remove a threat and restore control of that country to its own people."

Panama – In 1903, the nation of Columbia rejected an American treaty to build the Panama Canal, which was viewed by the American government as critically important to its trade and military interests. That same year, the American government supported a movement for Panamanian independence. After Panama established its independence, the United States could then move in to build their canal.

For much of its early history, Panama was controlled by 10% of its population, primarily people of European descent. A popular Panamanian leader by the name of Omar Torrijos, lead a coup securing some measure of power for the native non-white population. Tragically, however, Torrijos died shortly after taking power in a plane crash.

Manuel Noriega eventually came to power in Panama in 1983. Noriega was a drug criminal and election fixer that had been a paid cohort of the United States intelligence community, and was well known by the American government to be involved with drugs and violent election fixing as far back as 1972. In fact, in 1983 a United States senate committee concluded that Panama was a major drug money laundering and trafficking center.

Despite these facts, during this time period American government officials continued to protect and even praise Manuel Noriega. This was because Noriega was helping the United States government with its war in Nicaragua (for more details regarding this conflict, see Nicaragua section), and he was generally serving the American government's interests.

By the mid-1980s, the relationship had soured between Noriega and the American government. The government turned on Noriega for a number of reasons including his slowness in supporting America's war in Nicaragua, and his interference with American business interests. Another consideration was the fact that beginning in 1990, American control of the Panama Canal would be transferred to the Panamanian government.

Notes on the State of America

The American government began its attack on Manuel Noriega with illegal economic sanctions devastating the Panamanian population. This was followed by an attempted military coup that failed.

The United States government, as it has commonly done on previous occasions, embarked on a campaign to use the American media to vilify and demonize Noriega among the American population. Noriega was depicted as a corrupt, brutal tyrant. However, not only was Manuel Noriega the same person as when he was an "ally" of the United States government, he was a mild tyrant when compared to other brutal tyrants in neighboring countries.

However, as has happened many times before and since, the American government singled out Manuel Noriega so that the government could build a case among the American and world population that an invasion of Panama was necessary. In 1989, America proceeded to invade Panama using 26,000 troops, and killing hundreds or perhaps thousands of Panamanian civilians.

After the Panama invasion, the United States government passed a $400 million aid package (funded by the American taxpayer) for Panama, of which roughly ½ was money given to a variety of American businesses in the form of repaid outstanding loans, and private sector loans and guarantees. For more discussion on this topic, see Corporate Subsidies and Supports section.

The United Nations Security Council introduced resolutions on two different occasions condemning the American invasion of Panama. However, because America is a permanent voting member of the Security Council (to see how the process works, see the United Nations and the Security Council section), it vetoed and killed the resolutions on both occasions. This powerful veto power is not available for most countries in the world, particularly poor countries.

An ex-United States Army Ranger who participated in and witnessed the Panama attack was shocked at the wide discrepancy between what actually happened during the Panama invasion (destruction of civilians, their homes, their few possessions, and their critical infrastructure), and how the invasion was portrayed in news reports to the American people.

Most Americans are unaware that since the invasion of Panama by the American government, the country has deteriorated under the new rule of the American-backed administration.

Unemployment has skyrocketed to 35%, and employee pension rights and other benefits have been lost. Media stations were shuttered by American occupation authorities, dissenting newspaper editors and reporters were jailed or detained, and all political party leaders considered "leftist" were jailed or detained.

Local labor leaders were removed from their elected positions, and public employees that did not support the invasion were purged. Crime and poverty have climbed dramatically, homelessness and corruption is more widespread, and there is more money laundering and drug trafficking than occurred under Manuel Noriega.

Philippines – As America continued to claim widespread global military victories during execution of the Spanish American War, American military rule in the Philippines eventually transformed to American civil rule. The native Philippine people decided to resist the American occupation of their land and ended up fighting a 3-year war with America. American forces ultimately slaughtered at least 200,000 civilian Philippine natives (estimates have even exceeded 800,000 civilian natives).

The Philippine people were at this time viewed by the American public as inferior and infantile. It was during this time that Rudyard Kipling, a prominent poet, published the poem "The White Man's Burden". The poem essentially endorsed a sentiment prevalent in America at the time that legitimized American imperialism and global aggression by portraying the aggression as the white man's responsibility to save the poor non-white people of the world, and to protect America from dangerous enemies.

Real democracy in the Philippines came very slowly, and only when the American government had secured its coveted strategic military and trade interests. In fact, it was fully 15 years before local civilian legislators were elected, and independence from America was not granted to the Philippine people for 45 years.

Later, during World War II, the American government recruited Filipinos to fight for America by promising American citizenship and veteran benefits to new recruits. However, when the war ended in 1946 and in an example of deceitful twisted logic, the American government voided the offer for citizenship and veteran benefits thereby reneging on their promise. Some American Congressmen even had the audacity to suggest that native Filipinos pay the United States for their island's "liberation" from the Japanese.

Hawaii – Historically, the native population of these Pacific islands were devastated by diseases introduced by European foreigners. These diseases included cholera, influenza, mumps, measles, whooping cough, and smallpox. When Captain Cook arrived from Europe in

1778, the native Hawaiian population was 300,000. By 1890, the population plummeted 90% to only 35,000.

In Hawaii, foreigners dominated commercial enterprises. This factor strongly influenced the direction of the country. For example, American Sanford Dole ran a large pineapple plantation empire, and Claus Spreckels business interest was in beet-sugar.

In 1893, a group consisting primarily of prominent foreign business leaders launched a coup to dethrone Queen Liliuokalani. Subsequent events led to American Congressional legislation institutionalizing a new Hawaiian government, and imposing laws essentially consolidating power almost exclusively among the minority foreign business interests.

The result was the establishment of the Republic of Hawaii with Sanford Dole as its first President. In time, the American government wanted to own Hawaii outright so that the American government could eventually secure the Philippines (which is also in the Pacific region) as a territory while they fought their battles with Spain over control of Cuba. Commercial business interests as well as the desire to secure trade routes added to the movement for Hawaiian annexation.

Under the eventual annexation of Hawaii by the United States, the citizens of the then Republic of Hawaii automatically became citizens of the Territory of Hawaii and hence citizens of America. However citizenship was not extended to large numbers of people of Asian descent because they had already been excluded from citizenship by laws under the Republic of Hawaii.

It is interesting to note that when America entered World War II after the Japanese attack on Pearl Harbor, the Hawaiian sugar and pineapple plantation owners lobbied and were allowed by the American government to keep Japanese plantation laborers instead of sending them to Japanese internment camps (which was the law as specified by President Roosevelt's executive order – see Internment of the Japanese, Italians, and Germans section). This is another example of how American big business interests have often been conveniently exempted from national laws, or have even initiated and created laws that are intended to govern themselves.

Nicaragua – Historically, the American government has intervened twice in Nicaragua between the years of 1900 through 1933. In 1926, 5,000 American marines were sent to Nicaragua to counter a revolution. The American military force remained in Nicaragua for 7 years.

Later, during the late 1970s, a dissident group called the Sandanistas challenged the rule of a tyrant by the name of Somoza. The American government was uncomfortable with this budding movement, so a number of solutions were attempted to disrupt it. Eventually, the United States government settled on a plan to support Somoza and his brutal and sadistic national guard organization. By 1979, over 10,000 people had been slaughtered by neighborhood bombings. The American ambassador to Nicaragua at the time recommended to the White House that it should not try to stop the bombing.

During this period of time in Nicaraguan history, common Nicaraguan people were exceptionally committed to instituting a governing system that would improve the lives of all people, promote a sharing of national wealth, and encourage active grassroots participation in the country's development process.

Eventually, Somoza fled the country. However, he left Nicaragua bankrupt and war-ridden. In order to protect its interests in the Nicaraguan regime, the

American government organized the Nicaraguan national guard under the command of neo-Nazi Argentina military commanders and renamed the group the Contras or "freedom fighters". The United States government used this newly established group to wage a terrorist war against Nicaraguans.

The America government initiated harsh economic actions against the Nicaraguan people, and intimidated other countries into supporting American actions.

American government officials also vilified the Sandanista's populist movement. The United States CIA directed the installation of explosive mines in Nicaraguan ports. Additionally, through a series of financial actions by the World Bank and Inter-American Development Bank, and by disrupting fair democratic voting by Nicaraguans, the American government strove to retain control of the country and by extension the region.

During this time period, the American government allowed and even supported mass Nicaraguan civilian deaths. One of the continuing legacies of American policy in Nicaragua are the ongoing deaths of poor Miskito Indians (100,000 according to one estimate). Nicaragua has also become a major drug trans-shipment center.

According to the testimony of many people in 1986, including a former National Security Council staff member by the name of Lieutenant Colonel Oliver North, the United States government had for years illegally (in violation of congressional limits on such support) sold weapons such as wire-guided missiles to Iran in trade for the release of American hostages held in Lebanon. The United States government would sell the weapons through its ally, Israel, and the profits from these weapons sales would be secretly funneled to fund the American Contra

War against the Sandanista government and populist movement in Nicaragua.

This activity was essentially a covert use of illegal American weapons profits to support United States government control of Nicaragua and its surrounding region. The United Nations World Court (International Court of Justice) condemned America for its actions in Nicaragua.

Grenada – This is a small country with only about 100,000 people. There was a low-level social revolution occurring in Grenada that concerned the American government. In 1983, the United States government invaded Grenada with the following justification. The chairman of the American Joint Chiefs of Staff said (in seriousness) that the reason for the invasion was because the people of Grenada might impede oil shipments from the Caribbean to Western Europe, which might then prevent the America from defending Western Europe from any possible Soviet Union invasion. Therefore, the United States government dispatched 6,000 American troops to Grenada to overpower a few dozen paramilitary.

Somalia – From 1978 through 1990, the American government was the source of primary support for Siad Barre, a brutal Somali tyrant. During his reign, Siad Barre destroyed much of the Somali civil and social structure. He is also estimated to have killed 60,000 people. Nevertheless, the American government had strategic military bases in Somalia serving as a valuable point of deployment to the oil rich Middle East region of the world. During this time period, American forces are known to have themselves killed Somali civilians, with deaths estimated in the thousands.

On International Aggression

From 1983 to 1988, America supplied Siad Barre "the mad dictator" with 155 Howitzers, 20mm Vulcan air defense guns, light artillery pieces, mortars, anti-tank rocket launchers, firearms and ammunition. Despite this aid, by 1989 the impoverished country was in open revolt which forced Barre to flee the country.

In 1993, the American government decided to intervene directly in Somalia, ostensibly to hunt down one of the prominent warlords, and to be hailed as a deliverer of peace and humanitarian aid to the region. The American government launched a brutal military attack on a house where Somali tribal elders met. Somalis remembered this act, and when the American government sent its military into Somalia to hunt down the warlord, the result was a military debacle publicized as the "Black Hawk Down" military operation leaving 2,000 Somalis and 19 Americans dead. American military corpses were dragged through the streets of Somalia.

Unfortunate for the invading American soldiers, Siad Barre had left much of his cache of American weapons in Somalia. These same weapons were then used by warrior clans to bring down the American military operation. This debacle ultimately resulted in the additional deaths of 70 American and United Nations humanitarian troops. Thousands of Somali civilians died in this invasion and at the edge of famine, Somalia still swims in a sea of American weapons.

Sudan – In 1998, ignoring all existing protocol and international law relating to military engagement in foreign territories, and based on a belief that the action was legitimate retaliation for previous terrorist attacks, the United States government fired intercontinental ballistic missiles into the sovereign nation of Sudan to destroy a facility believed by the American government to be a production site for chemical weapons.

Post-attack investigations revealed that the facility was a pharmaceutical plant that manufactured and supplied about 50% of essential health care drugs for the citizens of the poor nation, including treatments for tuberculosis and malaria. The financial damage alone was $100 million, a massive amount of wealth to an already poor country. Five Sudanese were reported seriously injured in the attack. The facility manager even noted that machinery in the factory was imported from the United States, Britain, Sweden, and Switzerland. Finally, the United Nations itself confirmed that the facility had been legally shipping medicine to Iraq under the food and medicine for oil program.

Unsurprisingly, many citizens of neighboring Arab countries reacted with shock and anger, fueling even more popular support for future violence against America.

British Foreign Secretary Robin Cook was harshly criticized for standing by and allowing this attack to proceed. Many characterized the attack as an act of American "state terrorism" with British complicity. It is interesting to note that a number of years later, during the Iraq War, Robin Cook eventually resigned his British post to protest the British government's actions relating to events leading up to and during the Iraq War. He since has testified to British parliamentary committees investigating the Prime Minister's actions in the events leading up to the Iraq War.

Regarding the American government missile attack on Sudan, one might legitimately ask, "How would America likely respond if another nation sent missiles into our land and air space and destroyed an American facility?" And, "Why couldn't Sudan respond in a manner that America would?" And, "Is it moral and even smart in the long-term to promote a might makes right American foreign policy doctrine?" Finally, does this incident have anything to say with regards to those biblical proverbs "Do unto others as you would have others do unto you", or "You Reap what you Sow"?

Israel – America has been in many important ways involved in the Israeli-Palestinian conflict, and the American government is clearly not an unbiased party with respect to the ongoing Middle East conflict.

The American government was instrumental to the establishment and recognition of the Jewish state of Israel in the aftermath of World War II. Important Middle East national borders were defined post-World War II, primarily by the British and American governments to satisfy their particular business and strategic military interests. It is in this context that the state of Israel was born in the middle of Arab territories.

Since that time, the United States government has had a strong partnership with Israel. America provides $3.1 billion per year in military aid to Israel. This is by far the largest amount of military aid America gives to any country in the world. The United States gives about $1.3 billion to Egypt, $226 million to Jordan, $52 million to Bosnia Hercegovina, and $33 million to Yugoslavia (Kosovo). This type of aid is in the form of military grants, loans, weapons, equipment, and technology.

The United States also gives Israel about $1 billion per year in the form of economic aid. These aid packages to Israel are actually illegal according to 1977 United States foreign aid legislation barring foreign aid to countries secretly developing nuclear weapons. Finally, Congress also recently approved $9 billion in loan guarantees, and an additional $1 billion to cover expenses related to the Iraq War.

Israel has not formally declared its possession of nuclear weapons because it is not a signatory to the nuclear weapons non-proliferation agreement. However, it is widely estimated that Israel possesses 100 to 200 weapons of this type, as well as chemical and biological weapons technology.

Israel also has had a history of violations with respect to numerous United Nations Security Council resolutions, including a 1978 resolution regarding Israel's illegal occupation of southern Lebanon. Israel currently occupies a foothold in Southern Lebanon called the "security zone". This zone is controlled by a mercenary army called the South Lebanon Army, and is backed by the Israeli military. According to reports, the actions by this army have been brutal, and they have included massacres and the use of torture chambers.

Since the country's founding, Israel has continued expansion of its territories. A major annexation of land occurred through a major Israeli-Palestinian war in 1967. Since then, Palestinian populations have embarked on a formal resistance movement against what has largely been viewed as an Israeli occupation of disputed territories, and the continuing spread of Israeli settlements. In the past decade, the Israeli population in the disputed West Bank and Gaza Strip alone has doubled from 115,000 people to 220,000 people.

Because Israeli military strength is so overwhelmingly strong compared to Palestinian military strength, the Palestinians have had to use guerilla tactics and desperate suicide bombings to resist. Attacks on both sides have resulted in a continuing stream of deaths and injuries. There are almost daily Israeli attacks and targeted assassinations on Palestinians in the West Bank and Gaza Strip regions (estimated 2,300 Palestinians killed to date), and more than 100 Palestinian suicide attacks (estimated 360 Israelis killed to date). There are also documented reports and testimonies relating to Israeli military use of chemical weapons on Palestinians.

By no measure are Israelis, or those of the Jewish faith living outside of Israel, monolithic in their individual views toward the Israeli-Palestinian conflict. There are widely differing opinions among the Jewish populace both inside and outside of Israel.

In a strange twist, in the United States there is ardent support for Israel's claim of the disputed territories among fundamentalist Christians. They believe that the Jewish people must occupy the territories prior to the apocalypse predicted in the Book of Revelation (A final great battle accompanied by the coming of God). This apocalyptic event requires that the Jewish people ultimately either change their religious beliefs or perish.

Thus, fundamentalist Jews and fundamentalist Christians (including those within America) are in a strange alliance with regards to the defeat of the Palestinian claim to territories in the Middle East. Even the United States Congressional House Majority Leader is a member of this category of people. It has been estimated that 15 million people form the core of this Zionist fundamentalist Christian movement in America, and that 15% of the American electorate belong to related evangelical churches.

In the United States, a powerful pro-Israel lobbying group, the American Israel Public Affairs Committee (AIPAC), has donated large sums of money to politicians and clearly have close relationships and strong ties with American political leaders.

Afghanistan – The American government equipped and funded probably the largest Islamic Jihad in recent history. During 1980 through 1989, the CIA funded and armed what was then described as "freedom fighters against the Soviet Union communist invasion", but was by all accounts a Jihad war.

This covert support by the American government was envisioned and organized by a congressman from Texas, Representative Charlie Wilson, who held powerful influence over the House Appropriations Committee. Representative Wilson worked closely with a CIA operative and other people with very specific expertise. As a group, they were able to quickly establish unnumbered Swiss bank accounts for the United States government, dispense demolition expertise, and dispense arms and military training to the fighters in Afghanistan.

Largely unknown to most American citizens, taxpayer funds spent by the American government in Afghanistan rocketed from $40 million to an astounding $1 billion per year in funds and weapons. The weapons that were supplied started as small rifles, AK-47s, and machine guns, but quickly graduated to massive smuggling operations involving expensive and sophisticated weapons estimated at upwards of 65,000 tons.

The result was the arming and training of over ½ million Muslim fundamentalist fighters, including a core group of 150,000 "techno holy warriors" trained by the American CIA in the "art of urban terror". This is the war arena in which people like Osama bin Laden and the Mujahideen acquired arms and learned additional war skills.

In summary, America funded, armed, and trained the very "terrorists" that now threaten the country and the world. Apparently, in the 1980s it was deemed morally acceptable by American government and military policy makers to engage in this covert activity without the knowledge or consent of the American people who were paying for it. And in sheer irony, the American government now demonizes the very people they themselves funded, armed, and trained to perpetrate violence on other nations and peoples on behalf of American interests.

It is with this unsavory history that the United States government embarked in a blanket bombing military campaign in Afghanistan, in violation of international law to demonstrate tough retaliatory action for the tragic September 11 terrorist attacks. The bombing in Afghanistan could be characterized as essentially an American government temper tantrum after the September 11 tragedy.

The declared objectives of the bombing campaign were to root out leaders such as Osama bin Laden and destroy the Taliban regime suspected of supporting him. Osama bin Laden was never found, thousands of Afghan civilians were killed in the American bombing, and American forces continue to occupy and fight in Afghanistan as Taliban forces remain and at times resurrect in the territories.

As of July 2003, America spends $10 billion in taxpayer money annually in Afghanistan, a large part of which is spent maintaining a military force of approximately 9,000 American troops.

Iraq – Historically, American administrations have rebuffed democratic movements in Iraq, and even blocked

155

American Congressional denunciations of atrocities committed by Saddam Hussein. The American government, in fact, provided materials and support (for much more detail, see Saddam Hussein's Weapons Supplier section) to Saddam Hussein and his military for his genocidal actions against the Shites in the south, and the Kurds, Turks, and Assyrians in the north. The estimated death figures range from 50,000 to 100,000.

During the 1989 Persian Gulf War to repel Iraq's invasion into Kuwait, American armed forces destroyed critical Iraqi water and sewage infrastructure in clear violation of international law. It is estimated that the American military operation is directly responsible for up to 15,000 civilian Iraqi deaths, not to mention the deaths post-Persian Gulf War where more than 500,000 Iraqi children are estimated to have died from malnutrition or lack of medical attention, in large part because of American government imposed economic sanctions.

It has also been estimated that American government obstacles to Iraqi reconstruction post Gulf War, via sanctions and embargoes, resulted in 1 million mostly child deaths from gastro-intestinal disease. Even the United Nations was been highly critical of the American trade sanctions.

Unknown to most Americans, in the Summer of 2002, the United States military discreetly moved beyond simply "enforcing the no-fly zone" in Iraq, and embarked on an organized military bombing campaign called "Operation Southern Focus". This formal military campaign involved the use of 600 precision-guided bombs on 400 Iraqi sites that were suspected military fiber optic communications centers and military command centers. It can therefore be argued that this was the real beginning of the Iraq War.

Shortly after the blanket bombing of Afghanistan by American military forces, the American President identified 3 specific countries as evil: Iraq, Iran, and North Korea.   The President continually shifted his reasons to justify a military attack on Iraq. The reasons ranged from possession of illegal weapons-of-mass-destruction, to Iraq links to terrorism, to regime change of an evil tyrant, to liberation and freedom for Iraqi people, to exporting democracy to Iraq.   Governmental communications even suggested a link between Iraq and the September 11 terrorist attack.

During this time period, an overwhelming majority of countries in the world, and particularly the common citizens, opposed the impending war.   There were numerous mass protests throughout the world, and even within the United States opposing the war. 10 million to 30 million protestors marched on seven continents in one weekend alone.   In the months prior to the start of America's invasion of Iraq, 2/3 Americans, 7/8 British citizens were against the war.

Many people from countries in the Middle East region despised Saddam Hussein, but most Middle Easterners did not consider Saddam's regime to be an urgent or even substantial threat because Iraq had been decimated in the previous Persian Gulf War, and the country was suffering from subsequent harsh economic sanctions. A majority of religious leaders throughout the world also denounced the American government's march to war. People throughout the world understood that it was not the issue of the Iraq War exclusively, but rather that the American government's march to war was symptomatic of a dangerous change in America's use of its military power.

Also of interest were opinions originating out of the African continent regarding the American government's aggression voiced by arguably one of the most respected leaders in Africa and the world community, and a former South African President. With regards to America's march to war in Iraq, former-President Nelson Mandela said "For anybody, especially the leader of a super state, to act outside the United Nations is something that must be condemned by everybody." He then later also stated, "One power with a president who has no foresight and cannot think properly, is now wanting to plunge the world into a holocaust."

Prior to the formal American invasion of Iraq, in a 60 Minute television interview Saddam Hussein proposed that the American people and the people of the world be presented with a live international televised debate and dialog between President George Bush and himself. He argued that through this approach, people throughout the world could hear directly the perspectives from both parties and judge for themselves whether an attack on Iraq was justified.

In that interview, Saddam Hussein indicated that Iraqi civilians were already being subjected to American bombings. The 60 Minutes journalism team contacted the White House regarding Saddam Hussein's debate offer. The White House immediately and completely refused the offer. Thus, American citizens and people throughout the world were denied the opportunity to hear both sides of the conflict directly from the leaders without edit or restrictions.

By generating fear and through the effective use of the American media, the President was able to secure war powers and Congressional and Senate support to launch essentially a unilateral preventative attack on Iraq. Through its sophisticated media campaign, the American administration was successful in persuading a large portion of the American people that Iraq was an urgent danger and even somehow connected to the September 11 terrorist attack. This latter assertion was never validated, and is still considered extremely unlikely by most Middle East experts.

So, with unclear and shifting objectives, in violation of international law, without the support of the United Nations, without popular support worldwide, and against the spirit of the American Constitution that mandates that only Congress had the power to declare War, the President with support from the British government led America into a war with Iraq.

The war was short and ended within one month in early April 2003. The feared Iraqi use of chemical and biological weapons never materialized. To date, weapons-of-mass destruction (WMD) caches that the American government claimed that it knew of, either were not found or facilities that were found could not be definitively connected with WMD activity.

A post-invasion preliminary review of Iraqi hospital records indicate that in the battle for Baghdad alone, there were at least 1,700 Iraqi civilians killed and more than 8,000 injured. A preliminary count of total Iraqi civilian deaths is 6,000 to 8,000, many of them children, although the final number is expected to be much higher. Viewed from another perspective, America's one month Iraq attack has already killed 2 to 3 times the total number of combined innocent deaths to date of Palestinians killed by the Israeli military and Israelis killed by Palestinian suicide bombers (for these counts, see Israel section).

Upon completion of the "major war", America failed to live up to its obligations in Iraq under the Geneva Convention as a United Nations designated "belligerent occupier" for security as widespread looting, lawlessness, lack of water and food, lack of electricity, lack of medical care, unexploded bombs, disease and chaos predictably followed after the intense bombing and invasion by American military forces.

As Iraqis grew increasingly angry at the American invasion and extended occupation of their country, attacks on American forces continued after the major combat was declared to have ended. To date, upwards of 230 Americans have died and increases daily. The number of American military forces killed has already surpassed those lost in the entire Persian Gulf War. It is expected that American troops killed after the completion of the "major war" will exceed those killed during the war. And, not unlike Vietnam, American soldiers can no longer distinguish between friendly and hostile Iraqi natives.

Senior American military officials characterized the ongoing attacks on American troops as merely the dying remnants of Saddam Hussein loyalists, but they finally conceded that America was now engaged in a guerilla war. Meanwhile, at the same time the Pentagon proposed a cut in military pay for troops, including national guard troops, serving overseas in Afghanistan and Iraq. The cuts eliminate the paltry $75 per month in "imminent danger" compensation and $150 per month in "family separation allowances" for troops and their families already under severe financial pressure, many of them near poverty level.

The American government has indicated a desire to establish at least 4 military bases in Iraq (there are striking similarities to the sequence of events described in the Cuba section). The American occupying government has opened up Iraq's markets to foreign imported goods which has provided Iraqi consumers with lower priced goods, but has also devastated local suppliers and local jobs at a time when the country is already experiencing massive unemployment.

The American government is also considering a plan drafted by the Export-Import Bank and large American corporate interests to address Iraqi cash needs for infrastructure reconstruction due to the American bombing. It has been proposed that future revenues from the sale of Iraqi oil be pledged as collateral. Put simply, the plan is designed to use future Iraqi wealth in the form of oil revenues to pay corporations like Halliburton and Bechtel now to rebuild the Iraqi infrastructure destroyed by American military bombing. One might view the scenario as: America destroys the infrastructure, rebuilds it for a profit, and mortgages the future of Iraqis.

The only other alternative is for the American taxpayer to pay for the rebuilding of the Iraqi infrastructure, while also continuing to pay American military contractors to replenish the inventory of bombs that were consumed to attack Iraq.

The United States government has to date spent upwards of $50 billion of American taxpayer money on the Iraq War and occupation. American taxpayers face additional payments of at least $4 billion per month to remain in occupation with approximately 148,000 troops, and only if the number of troops in Iraq is not increased in the future. At the same time, back in America, the federal government is facing a $455 billion budget deficit and attempting to push the financial burden for basic domestic social programs onto already deficit-ridden states and local governments who simply don't have the resources to pay for them. Many social programs will simply die.

The American government continues to attempt to repair the massive diplomatic and credibility damage done with respect to America's relationships with the

United Nations, NATO, and most other countries of the world.

There have also been questions raised by senior officials in both America and Britain regarding the sourcing, interpretation, nondisclosure, modification, and use of intelligence information to justify the urgent invasion of Iraq. There is strong evidence surfacing that the United States President had already decided on military action in Iraq, while posturing to the United Nations that diplomacy was still a realistic and seriously considered option.

The United States National Security Council has conceded that the accusation that Iraq was attempting to acquire uranium from several African countries was based on a forged document. The President of the United States highlighted this accusation in his critically important State of the Union address intending to build support among the American people for his military action against Iraq.

And, while Britain citizens and political officials are investigating their own country's march to war in open forums, the American Senate Intelligence Committee decided to make its investigation and hearings closed to the American public.

And, in contradiction to the widespread belief by many Americans (a notion advanced by the President) that the invasion of Iraq was part of a broader war on terrorism, senior United States intelligence officials have since stepped forward to confirm that there was no established credible connection between Iraq and Al-Qaida, and thus the September 11 attack.

From the beginning, most Middle East experts were highly skeptical regarding the implied relationship between Iraq and Al-Qaida because Iraq's secular regime under Saddam Hussein was exactly the type of regime that Islamic fundamentalists such as Osama bin Laden and Al-Qaida wanted to replace. In fact, a United Nations terrorism committee had no knowledge of any relationship outside of what was being accused by the American government.

A previously classified National Intelligence Estimate document has been released and confirms that the American intelligence community, at the time of the President's speech to the American people, thought that it was unlikely that Saddam Hussein would give weapons-of-mass-destruction to terrorists unless he was facing death or capture and his regime was collapsing after a military attack. This would seem to imply that the Iraq War served to destabilize and make more dangerous both American and global national security.

Post-war, the American government has also been reevaluating trade policy with other countries based on their compliance in supporting the American government's war in Iraq. Countries will face uncertain trade negotiation outcomes as trade punishment actions are taken against those countries that did not defer to the American government.

One of the professed objectives of the attack on Iraq was to bring democracy to the country. Subsequent to the end of major conflict, the American government quietly dropped a highly publicized effort to set up an interim Iraqi political council as a first step toward Iraqi democracy. They retreated instead to keeping Iraq under direct American control, while hand picking a 30-person Iraqi board with an advisory role only. Understandably, Iraqi leaders were angered by this important reversal in direction.

Polls post-Iraq War indicate that in Muslim communities throughout the world, Osama bin Laden by an overwhelming margin is held in higher esteem with regards to world affairs than the American President, and Muslim communities strongly fear American attacks on their communities. In Western Europe, America's reputation has plummeted dramatically since September 11 (when America garnered the sympathies and support of peoples around the world). People in that region now believe that America in fact acts unilaterally with regards to foreign policy.

Under the present circumstances in Iraq unleashed because of the military attack, the American government has now returned to the United Nations, which it previously spurned, to solicit its help by contributing troops to help clean up and stabilize the situation. It finally became clear to the American administration that a more global approach, including the peacekeeping body and access to additional resources are required to give credibility to the American presence in Iraq.

American politicians from all parties are now voicing deep concern and outrage regarding the White House and Pentagon's justification, approach, and results from the Iraq War, and is questioning the war's relationship to the "war on terrorism". Although varying and unpredictable, estimates of the ultimate costs to the American taxpayer for the Iraq War and occupation have reached as high as $600 billion.

And now, in an apparent replay on history, senior American government officials have begun to publicly vilify Iran, North Korea, and China characterizing these countries as urgent threats to America and the world.

Americans are also questioning why the White House will not disclose the content of 27 pages from the Congressional report on the September 11 attack. While some experts speculate that the content might expose involvement in the terrorist attack by United States' ally Saudi Arabia, it is actually President George Bush that is refusing to disclose the information. Saudi Arabia has made it clear that it would like the information disclosed so that it can defend itself against potential charges and harm to their reputation.

On the Media

Chapter Summary – Despite its liberties and freedoms, Americans have arguably become the most entertained and marketed to population in the world, while becoming alarmingly ill informed on matters of real importance. This unfortunate state is the result of many factors, not the least of which are dramatic changes in the American media industry (television, radio, magazines, newspapers, movies), and how the media industry now operates in the United States.

This is not to suggest that there is a conspiracy among media companies or between media companies and the government (although there are certainly cases of media conspiracies and direct manipulation of the media). And, it is also not to suggest that there is not a freedom of the press. Rather, it is to suggest that the media institutions, the news organizations, the entertainment industry, and its owners are becoming largely one. Furthermore, these businesses are commonly motivated, organized, and operated in a manner running contrary to the aims of most thoughtful Americans.

Popularity and viewer ratings have historically been one of the most powerful drivers of American media (this measure, like financial profits, can be a highly misleading guide when considered by themselves). And yet many Americans have become increasingly disenchanted with the quality of American programming and news reporting.

For the most part this feeling of disenchantment has not been limited to any particular political or personal ideology. The sentiment is pervasive, and it is more related to the question of whether Americans can be entertained in a healthful manner, whether Americans have convenient access to truly important news of the day, and whether news and information is presented in a manner allowing the consumer to form a well-informed opinion.

What has not changed from the early years of American history is that the media continues to have a profound impact on society. This is the reason that the use of the public "airspace" has historically been considered a precious and regulated resource belonging ultimately to the American people. The people then grant, through its government, license for its use by media companies in which they are allowed to make a profit.

Like all humans, Americans are highly influenced by what they predominantly see, hear, and read in the media and among their community. Anyone who has sat as a juror in a courthouse has firsthand experience with the power of suggestion and influence. One moment, the juror hears the prosecution's case and is certain that the defendant is guilty. The next moment, the juror hears the defense's case and is absolutely convinced that the defendant is innocent.

Influence by external stimuli is a natural human process. And most Americans would probably agree that this power should be controlled in a manner that is helpful rather than hurtful to its citizens. Furthermore, the media must be held to a higher level of responsibility than other industries with respect to protecting the institution of democracy. This is why America's founders dealt specifically and deliberately with the media, or the press, in the United States Constitution.

Consolidation and Control of Media Resources – In North America by the mid-1990s, there were 7 major movie studios, 1,800 daily newspapers, 11,000 magazines, 11,000 radio stations, 2,000 television stations, and 2,500 book publishers. Of this resource pool, 23 large corporations owned and controlled over 50% of the business in each medium. In some cases, a corporation had a virtual monopoly.

Consolidation and control of the media has advanced even further during the past decade. In 1984, 50 corporations dominated American media; now it is only 10. In 1946, 80% of the newspapers were controlled by individuals and small independent firms. In contrast, today 80% of the newspapers are owned by corporate chains and 3 corporations own almost all of the 11,000 magazines. It has also been estimated that 70% of network programming on television originates from only 3 large media corporations.

Examples of large media corporations are Viacom, Clear Channel, News Corporation (Fox Media), Hearst Corporation, and Walt Disney.

This undeniably extensive consolidation of America's media resources has resulted in many of the same results on the market as other monopoly or oligopoly (a few dominant players) markets. These results include less consumer power with regards to prices to access information and entertainment.

However, perhaps more important than the market constraint on prices, media consolidation has resulted in fewer real choices for the consumer regarding the diversity and quality of the news and entertainment that they consume. There are millions of "brands", but these brands are fundamentally the same in content and even style. It has actually become harder for consumers to find real alternative sources of news and entertainment.

Media Techniques – It is important for people to be aware of common techniques used by the American media to deliver news and information to the American people and the broader world community.

Genuinely important news information is available in the American media, particularly in newspapers, but in reality it is very difficult to access. Important information is often located in a story that is placed in the middle or the back pages of the newspaper (in media parlance, this is called "burying the story"), or it is located at the end of articles (this is called "burying the lead").

The end result is that the vast majority of news consumers either never see this information, or they assign an inappropriately low level of importance to this information in comparison to news stories that are located prominently on the front page. This is how the media is able to strongly influence what Americans think is important, and how important it is.

This media technique is used every day by news organizations throughout the world as a necessary method for them to prioritize and organize news for consumption. The hierarchy in newspapers as relates to its stories is as follows: Front page headline (this serves essentially as a prominent billboard message), front page story, and then all the rest of the buried stories. The hierarchy within any particular news story is as follows: Lead paragraph, main body of story, end of story. These basic news reporting hierarchy rules powerfully define what is ultimately considered as important issues by the American people.

Another related media technique is a concept called "framing". This is how the information is presented: The assumptions that are implied by the writing, what information is emphasized, what is discussed first, what is discussed more extensively, and how the information is presented.

A simple example illustrates the concept of framing. Compare the following two questions: "Did Saddam Hussein attack America on September 11?" and "How did Saddam Hussein attack America on September 11?" Obviously the second question, as framed, automatically implies an assumption that Saddam Hussein attacked America. The framing of the question naturally leads the reader to conclusions. The use of framing powerfully influences how news is consumed.

Media bias generated through the use of these media techniques can never be eliminated. However, it is vitally important that measures be taken that provide Americans with convenient access to alternative points of view, so that these biases can be balanced with alternative perspectives. It is in this manner that news consumers can arrive at reasonable conclusions regarding important issues. Media diversity, which provides a measure of protection against this type of dangerous "group think", is critically important to preserving (some would say rapidly disappearing) news quality and basic journalistic ethics and practices.

Headlines and the Buried Real Story – A recent example that will further illustrate the concepts discussed in the Media Techniques section follows.

On June 1 2003, the San Francisco Chronicle newspaper had a front page headline stating "President Bush calls on Europe to Help Vanquish Evil". The front page story came complete with photos of the President's visit to Auschwitz, the infamous concentration camp in Poland. This front page story naturally evoked images of the holocaust under Nazi Germany, and the World War II battle between good and evil.

What could alternatively be considered the important story of the day might be a story that was reported the day before, buried deep within the newspaper, at the end of an article on page 14.

In that article was a photograph of graffiti in Europe that said "Bush go home". And, at the end of the article, it was reported that Poland's Mayor of Krakow Jerzy Majchrowski (who of course knew directly about tyranny and brutality because of Poland's history) refused an invitation to attend a speech by the American President.

The article reported that the Mayor, in a recent Polish newspaper column, drew parallels between the American President and the late Soviet Dictator Joseph Stalin. He further criticized the Iraqi civilian casualties resulting from the Iraq War. Mayor Majchrowski even suggested that American leaders should face a tribunal similar to the Nuremberg war crimes trials against the Nazi leaders at the end of World War II. He stated that "Stalin has been a great teacher", and that the American presidential administration has "put itself above the law".

For whatever reason, this was not considered a headline or even a lead in a story in the American media. In contrast, this type of story often becomes the front page headline or lead story by news organizations throughout the world outside of the United States.

This is but one simple example of how worldviews held by Americans can become overly biased and disjointed with how the rest of the world perceives America. Essentially, the media becomes a dangerous mirror whereby Americans can look and see what they want to see. Or, what others in the government, military, or big business want Americans to see. This use of the media has little to do with providing useful and relevant information on important issues of the day so that Americans themselves can come to well informed conclusions.

In this example, the natural result would be that many Americans would likely conclude that his or her government is (justifiably) leading a global fight against evil.

If one desires to avoid this type of "brainwashing", one must either avoid the media altogether, seek alternative or opposing perspectives, talk to other people (possibly from other countries) regarding their opinions, and learn to think critically about all information that is presented to them and how it is presented. This takes much work, and in reality this is why most people don't do it.

Most Americans are under unrelenting pressure to simply earn a living and to care for their families. In many cases, they do not have the time or energy to think about the broader American and world issues. And, for some Americans, they really don't care much about these issues and tend to focus on their own immediate concerns. In these cases, the American media essentially tells the people what is important and how important it is, and the people follow.

Another example demonstrating the power of front page headlines is the flood of front page stories that reported on the American government's efforts to establish democracy in Iraq by forming an Iraqi governing body. Most Americans were probably impressed with their country's noble efforts to bring liberation and democracy to the poor Iraqis. It was only a short time later that this front page story completely disappeared. However, buried deep within newspapers were short news stories regarding the fact that the American administration had quietly dropped the idea of forming a democratic Iraqi interim government. The American government instead kept governing power over Iraq for themselves, and instead simply hand-picked a 26-person Iraqi board with no decision making authority (advisory purposes only).

Americans Out of Step With the World – In recent years, it has become painfully clear to many Americans that their worldviews are increasingly out of step with much of the rest of the world.

There are two factors that might be considered related to this question: The "herd" characteristic in the American public, and the "dumbing down" of the American public due to the commercial nature of the media industry.

There is a theory among people who study the influence of American media on the thinking of Americans. The theory is that 20% of the American population is made up of the real opinion makers and directional leaders, while 80% of the population are essentially followers. It is the follower's job to simply follow, don't ask questions, only think about other matters not related to issues of real power, avoid discussing taboo subjects such as politics and religion, or simply go away.

The idea is that if the 20% of people can be convinced on a particular issue, that the ultimate effect is that the entire country will eventually follow. Therefore, the battle for popular opinion in America is really a battle to influence only 20% of the people.

The second factor relates to the fact that mainstream American media is an extremely commercialized animal, and increasingly even more consolidated and less controlled. The nature of the mainstream media is becoming like the nature of the fast food industry in America. It is more designed to give the consumer what they want (fast and tastes good) rather than what might be healthier for them (nutrition and balance). It is designed more for quick and easy mass consumption. It is designed more to titillate and entertain, rather than to educate or inform.

What has suffered is the depth of reporting and investigation, the diversity of coverage, and the variety of information and views that might conflict with the prevailing views broadcasted by an increasingly uniform mainstream media industry. In short, it has resulted in a real "dumbing down" of the typical American citizen.

An example of this phenomenon is that many Americans are unaware that most of the world considers America a greater threat to world security than any other country that America has deemed "rogue" or "terrorist" (this would appear to make sense given America's overwhelming military and economic power).

A majority of Americans eventually came to believe that Saddam Hussein and Iraq were an urgent and imminent treat to America's national security, while people in the Middle East overwhelmingly viewed Saddam Hussein and Iraq as a much less of a dangerous threat, largely because of Iraq's weakness after the devastation of the Persian Gulf War and years of harsh economic sanctions.

Middle Easterners are the people that one would expect are infinitely more knowledgeable about Iraq, and thus probably arrive at a more accurate assessment of the danger, than the typical American. They are the people that would most naturally have the reason to act against Iraq if there truly was a threat because of their closer geographical proximity to Iraq.

In stark contrast, Middle Eastern populations were overwhelmingly anti-Iraq War, while 66% of Americans believed that both Saddam Hussein and Osama bin Laden were responsible for the September 11 attacks, according to a 2002 poll by the Pew Center. There was never any evidence of Saddam Hussein's involvement in the September 11 attack, and it is a theory generally not believed by most Middle East experts.

A Frightened Population – Despite their country's immense wealth and power, the America populace is surprisingly terrified and frightened.

Some of this problem relates to the nature of news reporting in the context of the commercial interests of the American media industry. Increasingly, in order to survive as an "economically viable" entity, the media is inordinately focused on delivering news that grabs and holds the interest of the consumer, rather than delivering useful and relevant news in a balanced manner.

As a result of this pattern, Americans feel constantly besieged, whether it is by an evil foreign enemy, or by criminals, or by diseases. The result of this affinity toward fear inducing news is a frightened and anxious population, with less attention focused on truly important matters that are of a more chronic and less sensational nature.

Valid concerns relating to the state of American jobs, the economy, pensions, health care, education, culture and even the legitimacy of its own government leaders are continually neglected to deal with the perceived more "dangerous and urgent" issues of the day.

A specific example follows. After the events of September 11, 3% of the American population believed that Saddam Hussein and Iraq were an imminent threat to American survival. This figure rose quickly to 60% as more media suggesting this view was exposed to the American public. The end result was that two assertions with no basis in actual fact (that Iraq was an imminent threat, and that Iraq was related to the events of September 11) were believed to be true by a majority of the American public. And naturally, these public beliefs correlated with the public's growing support to go to war against Iraq.

This phenomenon of fear influencing largely on a public's appetite for war is not new or unique. It has happened time and time again, including in Germany during the rise of Adolf Hitler as he rallied support among the general public to invade other countries. Hitler used perceived enemies, imminent treats, national security, strong patriotism, and flag waving to generate fear, which would then deliver public support for his military aggression.

Media Bias – The media will always exhibit some level of bias and prejudice. Bias and prejudice can never be totally eliminated, although most people would agree that the media industry should always strive to minimize its effects.

Studies by a reputable media watchdog organization, FAIR (Fairness and Accuracy in Reporting) studied one example of this tendency to bias. The watchdog organization analyzed a very large amount of data from the popular televised news program "Nightline". Based on data from 865 Nightline programs which included 1,530 American guests on those programs, it was determined that 92% were white, 89% were male, and 80% were professionals, government officials, or corporate representatives.

One might think that these statistics are not alarming because what is important is whether reliable and credible information was broadcast to the viewers. However, it is asserted that these statistics are very important because it has been validated that like groups of people naturally exhibit common biases and prejudices. Put simply, a rich white male corporate executive is bound to view the world differently and think differently than a poor Asian immigrant who grew up in poverty. It is not difficult to understand this concept.

This study raises serious questions regarding the diversity, variety, validity, and usefulness of news information to the American populace. This may again be another factor that serves to "dumb down" the American people as it relates to news information.

Big Business – Aside from a relatively small number of very wealthy individuals, large corporations are virtually the only entities with enough money to assert its voice in American government (for more discussion on this state of affairs, see the Money and Democracy section). A large corporation can and does assert its voice to the government through a variety of means: Making large donations to political candidates, providing money to political parties, deploying expensive lobbyists to the national and state capitals, financing political advertisements or other forms of interest propaganda, cultivating personal relationships and contacts with political leaders and influencers, deploying large sums of money to fight battles in the courts, or by buying off anyone who has the audacity to stand in its way. The common American citizen and small American business is vastly under gunned relative to large corporations.

There are too many specific examples and comparisons to enumerate. However, one example is offered.

A recent report from the Annenberg Public Policy Center of the University of Pennsylvania discussed the results of an extensive study regarding what is known as "issues advertising". Issues advertising is an information campaign directed to the public, to legislators, and to various governmental agencies.

It's intent is to influence opinion with regards to a particular policy, law, or regulation. In the case of this study, the investigation confined itself to the Washington D.C. beltway where the President, Congress, and other governmental regulatory agencies are located. The real financiers of much of this advertising were not always easy to ascertain because some organizations are fronts for other interests.

However, through painstaking analysis of over 5,000 print and advertising ads, it was determined that a total of $105 million was spent during the 107th Congress through ads sponsored by 670 organizations. Over ½ of the spending originated from the top 20 of the largest spenders (most of the 2002 top spenders were also 2001 top spenders). About 72% of the 25 organizations that spent over $1 million represented business interests. Furthermore, advertising representing business interests accounted for a higher percentage of television ad spending than in print ad spending (business interests have the money to pay for expensive television advertising).

$15 million was spent on advertising relating to energy policy. 94% of that money was spent by energy business interests, with only 6% spent by environmental interest groups.

The only equalizer between corporate and individual power has been the basic precepts of government spelled out in the Declaration of Independence, the Constitution, and the Bill of Rights granting certain rights to the common citizen. Unfortunately, over time large corporations have managed to claim many of the same rights as individuals, at least in the eyes of the law (see Corporate Personhood section for more on this perspective). This has only increased the level of corporate political leverage.

Government and the Media – Walter Cronkite, a highly regarded CBS anchorman and managing editor, once wrote, "This precious inheritance of ours, the constitutionally protected right to know what our government is doing in our name, is under daily attack by those in government who would prefer to do their business in the dark." In this statement, Mr. Cronkite referred to the propensity of all governments to withhold information from its citizens.

Over time, the American government has grown increasingly sophisticated at using media power to garner public support for its ideas and agenda. The government has learned to use its strong competency in marketing and public relations to actively manage the American media industry and shape public opinion.

It can be argued that this activity has reached a level of sophistication where it can be regarded, at least in part, a science. This activity occurs both at the Presidential level and at the military services level (for some history at the Pentagon, see the Military and the Media section). The White House Office of Global Communications (www.whitehouse.gov/ogc/) manages this marketing and public relations activity at the Presidential level.

As discussed in the Media Techniques section, American public opinion is regularly shaped through millions of everyday and largely invisible journalistic and editing decisions. These decisions impact what stories will be covered, and the relative amount of attention they will receive in American television, newspapers, and magazines.

These two decisions are often highly influenced by what the government wants to make as an important story. The continual and intense media coverage of the American president gives substantial media power to the government (this is called the "bully pulpit"). Furthermore, pervasive media consolidation has made the linkage between the government and media even more perilous to American democracy. Perhaps at no other time in American history has it been easier for the government to widely and effectively broadcast its message to the American people. A simple example of this social dynamic follows.

American political leaders knew about drug trafficking between Latin America and the United States for years, and many American presidents had even openly supported known Latin American drug traffic leaders of state (e.g. Manuel Noriega in Panama).

In 1988, only 3% of the American public thought drugs was an important issue. In 1989, the United States President launched a major government media campaign through the mainstream media in order to highlight the drug trade. After the media blitz, the importance of the drug issue to the American public had shot up to 45%.

Thus, the American government quickly and effectively manufactured a new enemy: Latin American drug traffickers. This again gave the government a valid pretext for military (or other types of) action against a country or regime; all in the name of protecting its citizens from a danger or enemy.

This example demonstrates how the American government can and does manipulate the media to exert control over public opinion. As discussed before, the end result is that attention is diverted from genuinely important and largely domestic issues, while an increasingly frightened American public stands ready to relinquish more of their own civil liberties and grant more power to their government to undertake their military campaigns.

Military and the Media – An American core competency that is difficult for anyone to dispute is its marketing and public relations capabilities. From its earliest capitalistic roots, American industry has honed a formidable expertise in marketing, selling, and influencing.

The quality of ideas, however, should not be confused with the ability to sell ideas. Just because Americans are good marketers of ideas, does not necessarily mean that America has good or morally sound ideas. These are two entirely separate issues. Morality is a value, while marketing is a competency. America is indisputably strong at marketing, while the morality of American policies may be argued.

This marketing and public relations expertise has not been lost on the American military. The military has always tried to influence public opinion, but significantly more light was shed on this less commonly known activity through events involving Frank Stanton, the President of CBS during the mid-1970s.

CBS News broadcasted a documentary, "The Selling of the Pentagon" that presented the results of an investigation into the American military's use of taxpayer money to create and broadcast massive propaganda campaigns through the media. The campaigns were designed to increase public support for higher levels of military expenditures and for continued American involvement in the Vietnam War. The propaganda was clearly designed to "sell" rather than to "inform" the public.

Mr. Stanton was viciously attacked by the Pentagon for the documentary work, and even hauled before a formal Congressional investigation. These efforts to attack the CBS President were supported by the Nixon administration, which had a strong interest in sustaining public support for military expenditures and war escalation. After a long fight which involved a charge of Congressional contempt and jail time, Mr. Stanton prevailed in this one battle to protect the First Amendment rights of freedom of the press.

The Pentagon's marketing and public relations activities are arguably even stronger today. Extensive consolidation of the media industry has only served to make this activity even more effective in influencing and controlling American public opinion.

It could be argued that never before have American citizens had to work so hard to obtain balanced, relevant, and useful information regarding issues of importance. This problem is exacerbated by the fact that political leaders are increasingly dependent on the financial support of corporate military contractors to hold onto their elected offices. Furthermore, American citizens often feel unpatriotic if they even question messages that are being broadcasted to them by their government and military institutions.

American history is littered with examples of the military using the media to sell rather than to inform. A couple of recent examples follow.

Before the Persian Gulf War in 1989, a Kuwaiti girl testified to the United States Congress that she witnessed Iraqi soldiers tossing newborns from baby incubators. This testimony was trumpeted through the media, and stirred public opinion toward attacking Iraq. America went to war in the Persian Gulf.

It was ultimately determined that the girl's testimony was orchestrated by "Citizens for a Free Kuwait" which hired public relations firm Hill and Knowlton to sway American public opinion toward the march to war. The girl was later identified as the daughter of the Kuwaiti ambassador to the United States.

A second example is the extensive reporting on the American military rescue of Army Private Jessica Lynch. After broadcasting an apparently heroic and dramatic rescue of the private, it was determined through credible British BBC reporting based on interviews with first hand witnesses, that Iraqi soldiers were not even present during the rescue. In fact, it has been reported that Iraqi doctors and nurses had attempted to deliver Private Lynch directly to the Americans before the "rescue", but were forced to return to the hospital because they came under American fire.

This version of the rescue was much less dramatic and certainly less heroic than the version that was originally reported and promoted by the military establishment.

Deregulation of the Media - The United States Federal Communications Commission (FCC) recently voted to change the ownership rules pertaining to the use of the public's broadcast airways. The new rules significantly relaxed existing FCC anti-monopoly regulations. These changes are thought by many people to ultimately and perhaps rapidly lead to further consolidation of American media resources (for more specific statistics, see the Consolidation and Control of Media Resources section).

Even under the rules of the previous regulations, two large media companies, Viacom and News Corporation (Fox Media), were already in violation of the anti-monopoly market limits. As a note, in the years 2001 and 2002, Viacom, News Corporation, and Disney each contributed over $1 million dollars to legislators and they continue to aggressively lobby for industry rules changes.

The FCC chairman, Michael Powell (son of Secretary of State Colin Powell) led the FCC move to pass the new media industry-friendly rules, and did it with little to no public notification and input. Two of the five commissioners dissented on the action indicating that the change is of such importance that the American public must be adequately represented before a decision is made. Feedback collected by the two dissenting commissioners indicated overwhelmingly strong popular opinion against the rule changes.

Nevertheless, the FCC commission proceeded to pass the unpopular rule changes in favor of the interests of the media corporations. This issue received so much public outcry, that national legislators called for Congressional and Senate review of this FCC action.

On the Dangerous Triad

Chapter Summary – America has a crisis in confidence with regards to both its political and business institutions. This sentiment has been building for some time as Americans, as well as other people around the world, have experienced the now verifiable impact of global capitalism, the disheartening financial failures of large companies due to corporate corruption, and the pervasive feeling of separation between what American citizens want and what their elected governments actually deliver.

In this environment of public sentiment, Americans are also experiencing the very real impact of the rise of an age-old confluence of power: the "Military-Industrial Complex". This is not a new concept. This idea was described years ago in a speech by President Dwight D. Eisenhower, a prominent former American statesman and war general. He was a man who experienced firsthand the destructiveness of war. Upon leaving office, President Eisenhower said:

> "Understandably proud of this preeminence, we yet realize that America's leadership and prestige depend, not merely upon our unmatched material progress, riches and military strength, but on how we use our power in the interests of world peace and human betterment...This conjunction of an immense military establishment and a large arms industry is new in the American experience...In the councils of government, we must guard against the acquisition of unwarranted influence, whether sought or unsought, by the military-industrial complex.

The potential for the disastrous rise of misplaced power exists and will persist...We must never let the weight of this dangerous combination endanger our liberties and democratic processes...Only an alert and knowledgeable citizenry can compel the proper meshing of the huge industrial and military machinery of defense with our peaceful methods and goals, so that security and liberty may prosper together."

General Smedley Butler, an American World War I veteran commented in a 1933 speech,

"War is a racket. It always has been...A racket is best described, I believe, as something that is not what it seems to the majority of the people. Only a small 'inside' group knows what it is about. It is conducted for the benefit of the very few, at the expense of the very many."

These two excerpts make reference to a dangerous Triad – government, military, and big business – operating in a global market environment and increasingly under less control.

This is not to suggest that leaders of American big business, government, and the military gather in clandestine meetings to plan the country's economy and future war plans (although any study of history indicates that this can and has happened). It is rather to suggest that the current charged political environment, America's military strength, and the importance of money to the process create a very real dynamic resulting in nepotism and inordinate levels of influence by these three arenas of power working in conjunction on behalf of their own individual interests.

An analogy would be a slightly tilted roof that, by design, tends to drive most raindrops toward the lower side of the roof and eventually onto the ground. The roof design and the natural laws of gravity makes this so. No other specific intervention is required. Furthermore, specific intervention can be invoked to even further accelerate (or impede) this natural path of the raindrops.

Behavior resulting from this close association of power centers can and does exhibit consequences undesirable to the majority of people around the world. These consequences can ultimately include job loss and relocation, labor exploitation, human devaluation, increasing disparity of wealth, unstable financial security, prospect of armed conflict, less democracy, fewer real choices, permanent loss of priceless natural resources, and a reduction in genuine safety and security.

And to complicate the matter further, people throughout the world are now being challenged to develop appropriate responses to other relatively new global issues such as how to adequately and fairly manage the risks of controversial uses of chemicals and biotechnology in transnational food supplies, and of transnational bio-infections.

War, Money, Corporations and the Government – Some Americans understandingly want to believe that wars waged on behalf of their country have more to do with bringing a better life to others around the globe, and less to do with money. Unfortunately, the reality is that all war is powerfully and inextricably tied to money.

Aside from the obvious prizes that have traditionally motivated governments of countries to invade other countries (such as land, water, fossil fuel reserves, precious metals, and strategic military or trade locations), it is often overlooked by people that the very act of preparing for, waging, implementing, and reconstructing from war directly impacts the economies of the countries involved.

War is, in general, severely destructive to the economies of both the invading and invaded countries. National wealth is spent very narrowly to build weapons. This is wealth that is no longer available for developing and internally improving the countries. Countries then consume (use) the weapons to destroy assets and lives in other countries. And then after the war, countries must again invest even more future wealth to rebuild what was destroyed.

With regards to only the actual fighting phase of the war, $186 billion was spent in World War I. World War II cost $200 million per day using 750,000 planes, 280,000 tanks, and countless small arms and munitions. In more current times, with the average cost of fighter planes averaging upwards of $25 million each (with attendant missiles at $500,000 each), tanks costing $3 million each, and cruise missiles costing $1 million (300 missiles fired), the Persian Gulf War resulted in a $50 billion bill (a daily cost 2.5 times greater than in World War II).

Adolf Hitler and close friends and associates prospered financially by his war-mongering and military aggression. His country was poor and humiliated in the years following World War I, so he took the wealth from the countries that he invaded and from people within his own country. He pocketed the wealth for himself and his associates, or invested it into providing wartime jobs for common German citizens in order to encourage them to continue supporting his march to war. By 1944, Hitler owned 90% of the German press (valued at $2 billion), much of it confiscated from German Jews.

A relatively small group of large, politically connected American corporations are more often than not the economic beneficiaries of arming and deploying American troops, and then rebuilding the countries ravaged by American wars. This is American taxpayer wealth or wealth taken from the invaded country, that essentially flows into the coffers of the corporations that supply the war armaments, and secure the contracts to rebuild the devastated country.

Examples are too numerous to cite in entirety. An example from recent history is the selection of contractors to rebuild Iraq after the American invasion. Contract bidders that were included in a closed-bidding private selection list have been Halliburton (ex-CEO is the United States Vice President Dick Cheney), Bechtel (a company with a long history of high-level political relationships, including a board member who is an ex-Secretary of State George Schultz), and even bankrupt and accounting fraud-ridden WorldCom/MCI.

A subsidiary of Halliburton received $496 million in military contracts to repair oil fields and logistical work, which is effectively a recurring cash stream for Halliburton throughout virtually all phases of the Iraq War and reconstruction. Immediately after major combat in Iraq, Bechtel was awarded an immediate $680 million prime contractor rebuilding contract from the United States Agency for International Development (USAID) to rebuild Iraq's roads, ports, power systems, and schools. It is widely expected that Bechtel will end up with billions more in contracted work related to the Iraq War.

It must also be understood that even if an American Corporation like Bechtel hires local Iraqi companies to do Iraq reconstruction work, their net profit will depend on how much and how they compensate the Iraqi companies, which is frequently undisclosed to the public. Nevertheless, it is most certain that as the prime managing contractor (the main conduit for the money), Bechtel will reap considerable financial profits from the War in Iraq.

The American government also hired WorldCom/MCI, a company with deep relationships with the American government and military, to build a wireless phone network in post-invasion Iraq. This was true even though the company was recently bankrupted, scandalized for fraud, and has had scant experience actually building out a wireless network. This was part of a $45 million communications contract using American taxpayer money.

WorldCom/MCI's business with the American government rocketed to $772 million in prime contracts in 2002, which does not even include their numerous subcontract awards at both the federal and state level. These lucrative federal contracts occurs at a time when a federal judge and the United States Security Exchange Commission (SEC) fined WorldCom/MCI for fraud to American investors.

Essentially, American taxpayers will pay for WorldCom/MCI's fraud fine through the money that the corporation will earn on their Iraq contracts. The support of WorldCom/MCI with taxpayer money was a clearly inconsistent action, given that the American government has barred awarding contracts to bankrupt and scandalized Enron Corporation and Arthur Anderson.

As another example, Bechtel Corporation recently beat out Halliburton for a 10-year $2 billion contract from the United States military to destroy American chemical weapons containing mustard gas and various nerve agents at the Blue Grass Army depot in Kentucky.

This, again, is wealth that is unavailable for public investment to strengthen and improve America, including its homeland security. America's wars, therefore, profoundly and directly affect the national economy, employment, and indeed the state of affairs for future generations.

The economic benefits of war actually pay off for an extremely small group of individuals, and typically through the enrichment of the corporations that they own. Profits earned by corporations involved with wartime goods and services show up as increases in corporate stock prices, reinvestment into the development of future goods, or distributed to large shareholders and executives. It can be credibly argued that in today's American economy, the actual population of people that significantly benefit from wartime activity is a tiny portion of the total population.

In summary, wartime activity, whether justified or not, is really quite an efficient method to move wealth from the mass of Americans (through aggregate tax collection and high military budgets) into the pockets of a tiny population of Americans (through their significant corporate ownership, executive compensation, and consulting or advising relationships).

Defense Policy Board – America's government has a very high-level military advisory group directly connected to the Pentagon through the Secretary of Defense. The membership, agenda, and meeting records are shielded from public scrutiny (much like America's Competitive Council and Energy Policy Board chaired by the United

States Vice President). There is virtually no public information or oversight for these activities, and yet it is in those forums that key military, business, and energy policy and plans are influenced if not largely determined.

Nine of the 30 members of the Defense Policy Board have direct ties to companies that were awarded more than $76 billion in military contracts in 2001 and 2002. Four of the members are registered lobbyists, with one of them representing two of the three largest military contractors.

Members of the Defense Policy Board disclose their ties with private industry to the Pentagon, however these ties are not disclosed to the American public. Information that has been obtained indicate that the board is littered with people that have rotated between high level private sector and military contractor companies, and government or military service.

Diego Garcia – American history is littered with examples of the "dangerous triad" in operation. For other examples, see the On International Aggression section. The following story is but one specific example of how American government interests and military interests, largely on behalf of corporate interests, can come together to result in grave injustices. The story is of Diego Garcia, a coral island in the middle of the Indian Ocean.

In the 1970's, the United States government desired to establish a military base in the Indian Ocean because of close proximity to the Middle East and Southeast Asia. From this strategically attractive location, the American government would have a place from which to launch aircraft and dock ships in support of military operations in the various nearby geographic regions of interest.

It is logical that this need in part stemmed from the desire to support and protect American business interests in the regions, and to secure and protect valuable natural resource infrastructure for critical commodities such as petroleum products, if required in the future.

To meet this objective, the American government with support from the British government, secretly and summarily exiled an estimated 2,000 Diego Garcia natives who had prosperously inhabited the island for over 200 years. America and Britain worked together to forcibly relocate the entire native population over 1,200 miles away to the Mauritius and the Seychelles tropical islands.

To intimidate the natives into doing what was ordered of them, the British troops used American military vehicles to gas the native's pets to death. With no compensation or aid (the natives left their houses and possessions, and were only allowed to take one suitcase of clothes), these natives became squatters in a foreign land and lived their remaining lives in slums. Many natives fell into deep despair leading some natives to early deaths, including death due to suicide.

In a revealing memo between the American and British governments, a legal expert made reference to "maintaining the fiction" that Diego Garcia had no natives. To add insult to injury, America has barred Diego Garcia natives from returning to their island for any reason, including to visit the graves of their dead ancestors or to work on an American military base now located there. Presumably, this is because the American government and military fears that natives may speak out about the atrocity, or initiate a claim for return of their stolen land.

Britain's highest court eventually ruled that the action by the American and British governments was illegal, but the court did not grant any remedy to the natives. The natives continue to press their lawsuit against the two countries.

As a final note, for their support to the American government in this international crime, the British government received a $14 million discount from the United States on desired American-made Lockheed-Martin Polaris missiles for British submarines.

A Future for America

In this final section, the writer offers his own personal thoughts and suggestions regarding America's future for the reader's consideration. These are based on the information discussed in this book and the worldview and opinions of the writer. They are intended as the simple offering of ideas from a fellow common American citizen, and a citizen of global humanity. The reader may agree with all of the thoughts, none of the thoughts, or a few of the thoughts. You are encouraged to integrate these thoughts with what you already know and what you have learned, and draw your own conclusions based on your own personal values and morals.

In the first sentences of this book, it was suggested that the value of the information in this book was dependent on what the reader valued in life. This book provided historical and factual information pertaining to the United States that is less commonly discussed but is vitally important to know in order to form any useful opinion regarding important matters of the day. The information also put the United States in a global context, as a member of the international community and a member of global humanity.

Global Humanity

In most ways, the events discussed in this book are as old as human history. From the beginning, mankind has wrestled with issues relating to power, land, natural resources, war, atrocities, imperialism, human suffering, and poverty. But the current day differs in a few critically important respects: The very real possibility to destroy the world because of the shear power of current weapons technology, the ability to access global information almost immediately, and a very real choice that is to be made regarding the American democratic experiment. The choice is whether American citizens can bring the country's founding principles to reality, or fail to do so in which case the American democratic experiment will quickly end. America will simply become historically a brief failed experiment in democracy.

This is a choice that American citizens and the broader global community must make, and it will be made through both their actions and their inactions. Regardless of how powerful government and global multinational corporations are, they still cannot stop the will of the people if the mass of people are truly aware of their situation and they desire a different state of affairs.

American citizens are in a particularly advantaged position, and they bear a critically important responsibility regarding the future of the world. This is because they are a voice within a presumably democratic system of the most militarily powerful and economically rich country in the world. This responsibility cannot be ignored. How America conducts itself in its own domestic affairs, and particularly how America conducts itself with respect to international affairs, will bear greatly on the underlying culture and tone of the world.

Some Americans might be tempted to look only at the freedom and riches in their own lives, and conclude that there are no problems with America (and even feel intense pride in their country). It must be remembered that the internal freedom and riches that citizens of a country experience, are separate from how that same country can and does behave in the larger global community. It is not at all unusual for citizens of a wealthy and powerful nation (like the Roman Empire) to be personally comfortable and content, while the nation perpetrates predatory and violent acts on other nations and peoples in the name of national defense or other presumably moral reasons.

The United States administration has asserted that the current world conflict is a battle between good and evil. In fact, the administration has even self-righteously enumerated specific countries and people that are evil while inferring that the United States stands on the side of the good. From the information in this book, any reasonable and intelligent person understands immediately that evil is not the sole possession of any one country or people. Evil permeates human existence, including the United States.

Good and evil has more to do with individual values and worldview, how people choose to interact with other people, and how their interactions and actions ultimately affect all of humanity. These factors have no geographical or racial boundaries. Good and evil coexist in every human being.

And, because America's past is clearly littered with shameful actions and inactions does not mean that the world of the future would be better without America. It is to suggest, however, that the world would be better off to have an evolved America; perhaps different or more mature in action.

Because of its power and influence, America will become either a world force for good or one for evil. But two things are certain. America will be a potent world force. And, in the process, America will have no ability to claim ownership of moral authority with respect to actions by other nations and peoples until it has in the main addressed its own behavior. Behavior based on its own national value system and culture. If America can find a sustainable moral center the country has a chance of survival. If America cannot or will not find a sustainable moral center the country will perish. In the long run, the doctrine of "might is right" cannot prevail forever. America's colonial independence from the then immensely powerful British Empire demonstrated this fact.

This book revisited the "dangerous triad" of government-military-industry that had been warned against by United States President and World War II General Dwight Eisenhower. True to his warnings, this constellation of power has indeed reached a dangerous and toxic level. And, as predicted, it threatens the very core and fabric of the democratic doctrine in general, and America in particular.

State of Affairs

Is the danger of America's state of affairs exaggerated?

One need only open one's eyes to see the increasingly prevalent homeless, the working poor, people seeking work that pay a living wage, citizens woefully uninsured against the most basic of health risks, while a tiny minority live in incomprehensible wealth. And, the explosive disparity in wealth between the minority and the masses of humanity is even more pronounced when viewed beyond national borders and from a global perspective.

These most basic of concerns are not figments of imagination, or result from a state of affairs that are temporary in nature. They are the legacy of systematic historical American policy and behavior. When a government taxes its citizens and then spends one half of its discretionary budget preparing for, waging, and reconstructing from war, it is not surprising that the fundamental needs of American society are neglected and fall into severe disrepair. This state of affairs is not only morally wrong; it is unsustainable.

A more enlightened and sustainable direction for America is clearly required, perhaps more now than at any previous point in American history. And if this is to happen, American citizens must be able to move beyond the paralyzing fear resulting from government-induced or non-governmentally induced "enemies" or "threats". The specter of communism, corrupted Latin American drug traffickers, brutal dictators in Eastern Europe, evil religious tyrants in the Middle East, and nuclear aspiring Stalinists in Asia have been among the ghosts that have dominated the attention of American citizens.

George Orwell, in his essay on empire and nationalism said, "Actions are held to be good or bad, not on their own merits, but according to who does them. There is almost no kind of outrage – torture, imprisonment without trial, assassination, the bombing of civilians – which does not change its moral color when it is committed by "our side"…The nationalist not only does not disapprove of atrocities committed by his own side, he has a remarkable capacity for not even hearing about them." As seen from the information in this book, America has not been immune to these phenomena.

An honest appraisal of American history reveals that the United States has seldom acted internationally because they genuinely cared about freedom, liberty, democracy, human rights, and civil rights for the people of other nations. In the main, the truth is that America has acted largely to secure lands and resources for its own national expansion, and to strengthen strategic military and economic trade routes.

If there is a sincere desire to bring democracy, liberty, and freedom to other countries, then America should simply focus on making its own country a well-functioning democracy and a prosperous, fair, and sustainable society. Then America may serve as a powerful example. It is an insult to global humanity for America to attempt to market or "sell" democracy to other people, or to utilize an inflated military to force on others the adoption of American principles and practices.

If Americans truly believe in freedom, then Americans must also believe in the freedom of other nations to choose their own national values and governmental system. And if human atrocities and injustices do occur, a strong global institution of some sort is the only type of institution that will have any semblance of respect, validity or authority. Such a global organization would help the world community craft appropriate responses to global situations based on common human values. Of course, this may not be the easiest or quickest path to a response, and at times it may not satisfy all of America's interests. But this is, in fact, real democracy in action.

American Capitalism

However, democracy in America cannot be understood without understanding the underlying economic system of capitalism functioning within it. By definition, capitalism is the promotion of privately owned companies to accumulate and distribute profits in the context of a "free" market.

A Future for America

Capitalism as a practicing doctrine has historically focused almost entirely on the power of economic self-interest (return on financial investment). Because capitalism is such a powerful engine, it has the ability to promote both great prosperity, and to promote great corruption and exploitation. Like an engine in an automobile, capitalism must be operated under a system of control and constraint in order to be useful to society and to prevent destructive outcomes.

Furthermore, America will do itself a great disservice if it allows its citizens to divide only into two opposing camps: Flaming capitalists, or communist liberals. It is asserted that the solution lies somewhere in between. There is nothing un-American about suggesting control and constraints on unbridled capitalism. This concept has been expressed repeatedly by American citizens, and many persons of note.

An early founding American, Benjamin Franklin, was born modestly to a soap and candle maker. He did not have inherited connections to royalty or wealth. He was truly a self-made man of broad intellect and accomplishment. As Dr. Franklin matured, he became increasingly prominent and established many institutions designed not for private profit, but to serve the common good.

He encouraged trades people to meet regularly, solve common problems, and engage in general discussions. This was arguably one of the earliest colonial self-help networking groups. He suggested that Americans should "overthrow the sense of unbridled self-interest", and suggested instead that people would do better working and living together.

A fellow contemporary, Thomas Jefferson, believed that America should be a country where every citizen has an equal opportunity under the law to "modest prosperity". He did not say "infinite prosperity" or "unimaginable prosperity", but rather modest prosperity.

These two men considered the human value of greed, and suggested that it is in fact not good.

Mark Twain once observed of his fellow American countrymen that "some men worship rank, some worship heroes, some worship power, some worship God. And over these ideals, they dispute and cannot unite. But they all worship money." An American notion in the ideal should be that people matter, as well as profits.

Democratic societies are stable societies to the extent that there is a broad middle class. Human history has taught time and time again that if a society has an excessive lopsided distribution of wealth among its citizens, the society is innately unstable and ripe for social revolution. A society that has a small group of individuals who essentially own and control almost all the wealth of a country, while the masses of individuals cannot secure basic resources for life, cannot stand in the long term.

Here is a secret: Any capitalist worth his salt would conclude that the notions advocating service to the common good and broad dispersal of wealth are good ideas, because a true capitalist would understand the following rational.

When more money is put into the pockets of common people, they more likely than not will spend a hefty proportion of that money on goods and services that they require to fulfill basic needs for themselves and their families. Money that is left over may be spent on luxuries, or donated to charity, or put aside for savings.

A Future for America

In the United States it is commonly accepted by economists that two-thirds of the total national economic activity is the result of spending by common people buying common goods and services. This is called consumer spending.

If the mass of people are purchasing goods and services (including sexy highly profitable technology products), money will surely flow into the pockets of the wealthy class in the form of appreciating company stock prices and higher levels of corporate retained earnings (which companies can then distribute in the form of higher dividends to shareholders, compensation for executives and employees, or reinvestment into the company to develop more or better products and services). Furthermore, a strong economy allows for the ability to conduct public stock offerings, public financing, and acquisitions of growth companies, which would make any venture capitalist and investment banker blush with joy.

In summary, wealth will always fundamentally originate from the mass purchases of common goods and services by the many, rather than the limited purchases of highly priced goods by the wealthy few.

Most people are generally happy when they satisfy an adequate level of basic needs such as housing, food, healthcare, and education. These basic conditions allow a person to explore opportunities for personal growth. For the vast majority of people, these are adequate conditions for happiness. However, this is simply not true for people who are greedy or predatory. People of this nature will never be happy no matter how much they take from others.

In a popular American movie "It's a Wonderful Life", George Bailey, a common man argues with a greedy financier regarding the working people in his small town. Mr. Bailey had this to say regarding the common man, "This rabble you're talking about, they do most of the working and paying and living and dying in this community. Is it too much to have them work and pay and live and die in a couple of decent rooms and a bath?" Indeed, the key to sustainable economic vitality and political stability is a large and prosperous middle class.

Here is another secret: Businesses do not like uncertainty. And war is one of life's largest uncertainties.

Businesses thrive in environments that have levels of predictability and certainty allowing them to plan for consumer demand, and to invest for the development and production of products and services. As long as the United States has a government that is war mongering, the environment will remain unstable. Thus, businesses will not thrive and jobs will not be created for unemployed Americans (not to mention employment for people in other nations that are also affected by the global economic climate).

In general, wartime really benefits only a small group of individuals and companies. They are military technology investors, war profiteers, arms dealers, wartime advisors, and the relatively small group of employees of the companies that design and manufacture the military equipment and provide military services.

In the whole, war is hurtful to the economies of both the invading and invaded countries. Scarce national resources are used to destroy infrastructure and humans. Some argue that war is good for an economy (such as America in post World War II), but anyone who seriously studies what really happened often conclude that there are a large number of other factors outside of military conflict that really drove the economic growth. In war, infrastructure constructed over years is destroyed and eventually must secure financing to be rebuilt, and human lives are profoundly impacted with an incalculable social price that is usually paid for decades into the future.

Limited taxpayer money must be used for more constructive purposes, and in ways that benefit a larger population of Americans and lead to a truly more healthy and secure American and global future. Implicit in this thinking is the belief that the people's interests should drive the government's interests (because government is supposed to derive their power from the people), and that people's interests should come before the predominantly financial interests of global corporations.

Also implicit in this thinking is that resources that are common to the people should be protected and appropriately controlled as common national resources. If private industry is invited by the people to participate in producing or distributing the people's natural resources, there must be high levels of protections and control to prevent abuses. Americans need only look at recent history in the deregulated financial, energy, telecommunications, and media industries for stark examples of how control of national common resources can and will be abused by private industry.

Rule-of-Law

Also integral to this thinking is that "Rule of Law" that has no moral compass cannot stand in the long run. Americans must do everything possible to infuse moral principles into laws and the legal process, without unduly injecting partisan morality onto the American people. This is clearly a difficult task and requires painstaking attention to balance.

However, the law and legal system must be transformed from being a tool for the wealthy to force their narrow special interests onto the common American people, to a system designed to deliver impartial justice. And, America must begin to support and nurture international justice institutions, rather than seek to destroy them whenever they might be applied to the detriment of American leaders.

Member of International Community

The United States of America is a very young country; some would call it an early experiment in democracy. As such, American citizens have an ability to evolve the experiment into a healthy and sustainable country and doctrine that works in alignment with natural laws of nature and humanity.

However, in order to do this, America must transition from viewing itself as a superpower to viewing itself as a member of the international community. In this worldview, Americans must believe that the people in the vast majority of the world are more alike with respect to their human values and desires, than different because of their particular cultural differences.

This is a belief that essentially posits that all people of the world desire essentially the same things in life - family, friends, security, housing, food, water, education, opportunities to grow personally, and a chance to adopt healthy values and strive to do the right things with respect to fellow human beings. If America can assume a role and adopt the perspective of a member of the international community, there will indeed be dramatic implications regarding its future attitude, actions and behaviors.

This perspective will demand that America be more genuinely consistent with respect to its moral principals by demonstrating new behaviors and actions, rather than simply issuing obviously hypocritical rhetoric and public relations speeches. It is only in this manner that America can ever hope to serve as a credible moral authority with respect to democracy, capitalism, or any other philosophy or doctrine.

In doing this, America will be challenged to halt the simplistic behavior of supporting and eliminating leaders of other countries based, not on genuine moral grounds, but predatory self-interest. Self-interest is not necessarily bad, as long as it is not extreme and the process allows for real validation and fairness with respect to other nation's self-interest. This means that America might not get everything that it wants in every situation. And it certainly suggests that America stop depicting its self-interested actions as obviously hypocritical moral crusades.

Most importantly, this changed perspective requires a recommitment by Americans to strive for the realization of its country's founding principles. Americans must reaffirm that democracy by, of, and for the people is truly a desired result. And furthermore, that national wealth and resources must be redirected in substantial ways to projects that will really promote prosperity and security in America and in the world.

National Priorities (A Dollar Well Spent)

Every year, and particularly in times of economic hardship, America pits one group against another to fight over the scraps of money that remain in the budget after military expenditures. The debate always degenerates to what group is more needy than another, and whether to rise or to lower taxes.

Of course, some level of this discourse is necessary and should be ongoing. But, when viewed from a larger perspective, America has lost sight of the fact that the United States has a huge white elephant in our midst that profoundly impacts the country's implied values and spending priorities.

The white elephant is this: America is spending one half of its discretionary spending preparing for, waging, and rebuilding from war. And increasingly, federal spending is being funded by tax revenues from the people, and less from large corporations. Yet, it is the large multinational corporations that have the most influence over the very same national spending priorities that benefit themselves. The people are increasingly eliminated from the equation, both politically and economically. Many readers know this to be true.

Taxes should not be raised, particularly for the ordinary people in America who are already under severe financial stress. Tax policy for very wealthy individuals and large corporations should be reevaluated, and it should be publicly validated and acknowledged that both wealthy individuals and corporations inherently have enormous comparative leverage with respect to utilizing the political and legal system to their advantage. Therefore, it is openly expected that these groups continue to bear a significant part of the national tax burden.

Considering these factors, it is asserted that American military expenditures should be cut by 50% over a few years (for a perspective on military spending, see United States Military Spending section). This would still provide for $200 billion in annual military spending – an amount that is still 5 times the typical NATO country military spending.

Proponents of military spending typically defended America's obscenely high level of military spending by pointing out that various ratios, such as military spending as a percent of Gross National Product, have declined in recent history. This manner of viewing military spending operates under erroneous assumptions that simply because certain aspects of America's economy expand, that the government must logically expand (by the same proportion) the amount of its wealth that America spends on weapons to deliver equivalent national security.

Particularly with today's powerful and mobile weapons technology, these types of assumptions are not only wrong, but they are also dangerously misleading to the American people. Given the technological advances and the global nature of conflict in the world today, military spending can and should be significantly reduced while increasing the level of joint activities with global institutions, such as with the United Nations, to address military related problems.

It must also be remembered that America did not always have such an obscenely highly funded military. At many points throughout American history, military expenditures were quite modest. And, Americans have always been quite capable (thank you) to ramp up military expenditures and capability when believed to be under real threat.

A 50% reduction in military-related expenditures will free up $200 billion to help our states and local governments to strengthen homeland security, create jobs for Americans in more productive capacities (which will boost the economy), strengthen social security, reduce our budget deficit and national debt, and provide capital that will eventually lead to useful, valuable and potentially exportable new technologies and products. Under this scenario, the United States government could actually even consider a tax reduction for the American people, within a context that tax expenditures are being reprioritized while real community needs must also still be met.

Many new technology and products have historically originated through research and development military spending (for a detailed discussion, see Military Research Grants section). And, it is true that in many cases military projects have led to the development of valuable technologies that could be applied to other non-military commercial uses.

It is asserted that it is time for America to invest more money directly into useful non-military projects. These redirected investments of American taxpayer money will undoubtedly also spin off new technologies for useful commercial (perhaps even military) application. Notice that this spending approach implies a logic that is reverse from historical American policy logic. Investment is deliberately directed to useful and productive non-military uses, with the possibility that new technologies may be developed that have useful application to military capability.

Examples might include projects that directly advance homeland security, such as new technologies as applied to security at seaports, airports, and borders. Or, renewable energy and clean technology projects to wean the country off of its oil dependency (for more information, see Oil Interests section) and to preserve the natural environment.

These types of new technologies will undoubtedly be relevant and exportable to other nations, some of them in desperate need of this type of life-giving and stabilizing technology. These exports will also provide America with a future source of its own wealth. These are technologies that will serve to nurture and enhance global humanity, rather than to destroy and decimate it. Military capability will always be important. But, it must be at a level appropriate to the larger picture and it must be truly effective to the threats that it is designed to meet.

In this changed spending scenario, more money will be available to address those areas that have become all too familiar to Americans: Social security, health care, education, housing, reducing poverty, and paying down national debt. In general, most Americans support the concept of universal health care and improved education. Funds would be available to help the public and private sector to make these essential social improvements a reality, political and industry battles notwithstanding.

Strengthening homeland security, which is a real "defense" budget, might mean that America provides additional financial support for National Guard reservists and their families if they will be used in this capacity for a long time. It might also mean redeployment of military personnel (a sizeable, significant, and talented human resource) to support homeland security activities.

Many American military bases can be closed or downscaled, both domestically and internationally, with a negotiated and secured legal agreement to access and rebuild the bases as required if needed in the future. If Americans come to believe that a specific military buildup is required in the future, targeted war bonds can be designed to provide the required financing for these endeavors.

President Ronald Reagan said in his first presidential inaugural address, "No arsenal or no weapon in the arsenals of the world is so formidable as the will and moral courage of free men and women." This is a profoundly true statement. If America's land territories are ever invaded, or if the country's national security is legitimately in real jeopardy, there is no doubt in the writer's mind that the vast majority of American citizens (liberal or conservative, white or non-white, rich or poor, religious or secular) will rise to defend America and quickly organize to do so.

It is because the case for war in Iraq failed to meet basic requirements on so many levels that there was such wide division among people, both within America and with respect to the rest of the world. Contrary to what some Americans might think, people protested the recent war in Iraq not because they had nothing to do on a weekday afternoon, but because they collectively knew that the war in Iraq was a symptom of something greater that was deeply wrong with America and its interaction with the broader world community.

Strengthening homeland security might mean strengthening America's intelligence capability to vigorously, but appropriately and accurately, monitor and assess real threats. This capability is arguably more important than the actual numbers of American soldiers, planes, ships, tanks, bombs and guns.

New global threats might also include increasingly pervasive and powerful international organized crime networks, or to assess, understand, prevent, and combat risks associated with global biological infections (such as E Coli, Salmonella, Mad Cow disease, SARS, Monkey Pox, and numerous other microorganisms) that have real potential to become serious global threats, certainly economically if not only in terms of lives.

A Future for America

These biological threats remain because of profound changes in the food supply industry, such as the widespread use of antibiotics and the ultra-concentration of ranch animal populations. It is also because of the high level of movements of goods internationally and the pervasiveness of global travel. The threat from overseas infectious diseases is certainly not new to American history. Whole mass populations of American Indian natives were decimated from diseases introduced by early settlers from Europe to the American colonies and its western territories.

America can also then work hand-in-hand with all nations of the world to create and deploy a truly global intelligence and security capability, in the interest of and administered by a validated and credible global organization. In this scenario, global intelligence would then be more powerful, credible, and useful to uncover genuine security threats. Global terrorist acts against America and other nations can then be addressed, while real solutions are developed in coordination with other nations to address underlying root causes for the increase in terrorist actions, which logically might include poverty and oppression.

These are clearly not easy tasks, and they will most certainly face difficulties in implementation. But, a global response is the only credible sustainable approach to prevent and respond to any global threat such as terrorism. The onus of global security and peacekeeping, and the reduction and elimination of violent terrorist activity, must ultimately reside in the form of a united global effort. And, these efforts must address the root causes of terrorist actions.

To show good faith to a more secure world, America should immediately and dramatically reduce its own inventory of nuclear weapons by 90% over 3 to 5 years, while leading an international effort through the United Nations to denuclearize all countries in the world. In this same manner, all countries should be moved to reduce or eliminate chemical and biological weapons. It is only through its own example that America can claim the moral strength to be a leader in the global reduction and elimination of weapons-of-mass-destruction.

Domestically, the United States can shift its investments toward more positive future-related technology development. This can be accomplished by transferring research money from military-related projects such as those under the Defense Advanced Research Projects Agency (DARPA) and the numerous other military projects within the various branches of the armed services, to other critical non-military types of projects (such as renewable energy and clean technology – please make note that the writer is clearly not unbiased in this regard).

This redirected domestic investment will create new American industries and jobs for the future, develop technologies and products for future American export, and strengthen activity that will truly increase American and indeed global prosperity and security. The intention is not to halt American investment into new technologies, but to more directly invest into long term productive projects rather than destructive projects.

Also with respect to military weapons, it has been established in this book that America clearly has a strong, and in many cases a dominant role in providing weapons to the world. The argument from the weapons industry is that if America doesn't sell the world weapons, then other countries will and America wants a share of the profits. An additional argument is that America must have a strong weapons industry so that America will always have the most powerful gun in the world to protect its own national security.

America can't have it both ways. As long as it is a dominant user and seller of weapons, America has no ability to either preach to other nations regarding their possession and use of weapons and weapons-of-mass-destruction, or serve as a global leader of peace. If the 50% reduction in American military spending is implemented, America will defacto ratchet down its weapons manufacturing and supply activity.

Again, in this situation, a credible global institution will be critical to the eventual overall reduction in the global weapons trade. This includes both legal and illegal weapons trading, and may involve directly addressing global organized crime organizations. This includes the practice of trading weapons for other valuables such as drugs or precious minerals.

International Trade

America must not only act with regards to weapons policy. The country must also act with regards to its international trade policy, and its attitude toward global institutions and international laws and treaties.

America should validate the global community by using its power to strengthen credible but relatively young institutions and international agreements such as the United Nations (which America helped to found under Presidents Franklin Roosevelt and Harry Truman), the International Criminal Court, the Kyoto treaty (global environment protection), and the various weapons-of-mass-destruction treaties.

Additionally, America must critically examine its true intents with respect to its influence over and use of international financing institutions such as the World Bank and the International Monetary Fund, and international trade agreements such as NAFTA and CAFTA.

All too often, these institutions and trade agreements are used by the United States as a tool to exert severe economic pressure onto weaker countries and force them to adopt national policy decisions that ultimately devastate their own countries. As the richest and strongest country, America should strive to be an authentic example of a country that intends to help other nations develop economically while respecting their right to sovereignty.

Ultimately, these types of actions will lead not only to greater global security which will lead to real American national security, but it will also transform poor nations into wealthier nations capable of purchasing American goods and services. This will naturally lead to increased American economic prosperity and jobs.

In this spirit, America should reassess its international trade policy on a country-by-country basis. The United States should adopt a premise that it will intentionally and specifically open its large and wealthy market to imports from undeveloped and developing countries. In essence, run an American trade deficit with these countries. This action will serve to reduce the growing disparity in global wealth, and will also ultimately lead to real improvements in global stability.

Eventually, these developing countries will be in a real position to purchase more American goods and services (many peoples in developing countries love American goods, if they could afford to purchase them). At a point in time, these countries will be strong enough economically to further open their own domestic markets to American products, and allow for a manageable level of American investment into their domestic industries. This gradual but highly directed scenario will serve to prevent the hijacking of poorer domestic economies by American commercial interests, which ultimately leads to resentment and less global and national security.

However, the transition described in this scenario demands negotiating a delicate balance because America must also provide enough decent-paying jobs for its own citizens. Nevertheless, it is believed by the writer that a middle ground can be found that genuinely attempts to balance these two perspectives. A country-by-country, industry-by-industry, product-by-product analysis could help to identify the desired middle ground.

Finally, if America truly believes in justice and the rule-of-law, and if America expects leaders in other nations to abide by legal precepts and to be held accountable for acts committed by their administrations, then America must itself be held to the same standard. This implies that the American government must support credible, young global justice institutions such as the International Criminal Court (for further discussion, see International Legal Courts section). America will never be able to claim international credibly with respect to rule-of-law governing international behavior if it does not itself abide by the same rules that other nations are expected to abide.

Of course, the United States government is not responsible for all the bad things that have happened in other countries in the past. And of course, America cannot be responsible for every bad thing that is bound to happen in those same counties in the future. However, it should not be too much to ask that, in the future, the American government act and behave as a believable and credible advocate of democracy, freedom, human rights, and civil rights in its dealings with other countries by helping to support institutions that are designed to address issues of global justice.

At the very least, patriotic Americans are entitled to expect from their government that it would not be working to impede or subvert the authentic hard-fought freedom and democracy of people in other nations, as it has clearly done many times in the past. Even if it means that those countries do not become carbon copies of America, and even if it means that those countries will not fall prey to America's narrow business interests, and particularly if it means that the America cannot control the sovereign internal affairs of other countries.

America for Americans

On the domestic front, America has a long list of problems that have required urgent attention. For too long, Americans have had to accept from their political leaders that obvious critical domestic needs are not a national priority or have no real solution. This is a tragedy, as it is the basic domestic needs of Americans that lies at the heart of real prosperity and national security.

One of the best indicators of the real strength of a nation is its ability, or inability, to care for the weakest among them. Here the stark fact is that many of the homeless and many of the poorest among Americans are children. Children who grow up in harsh conditions usually become harsh adults. This results in a much bigger and more expensive problem for society. It can cost upwards of $30,000 per year to house a person in prison. Society suffers through increased crime, wasted lives, and a more dangerous living environment. It is easy to accommodate the wealthy and powerful, it is more difficult but far more important to care for the poor and the weak. Any family understands this concept immediately.

America must put in place social structures that have these aims. These social structures will not only provide care for the poor and the weakest of American citizens, it will have the added benefit of also noticeably improving the day-to-day lives of America's middle class.

More than any nation on this planet, America has the wealth to make universal health care a reality. This program would immediately and powerfully alleviate a very real fear for the majority of Americans.

The debate regarding universal health care has always degenerated to the question of who pays for it. The point to be made here is that whatever the additional costs, America is wealthy enough to do it given sane national spending priorities. And, if it means allocating a greater portion of the (taxpayer provided) budget to help fund universal health care for Americans, this should be done.

Not taking anything away from Bill Gates (founder of Microsoft) as a person or as a successful capitalist, but it is obscene when a single person holds more wealth than 125 million other Americans, or 45% of the population. Even to a diehard capitalist purist, this unimaginable lopsidedness in wealth distribution is not only questionable on face value, but it also undermines the ability of that wealth to be put to productive economic use within America. Rather than having this wealth broadly distributed within the American population and flowing throughout the American economy via spending, the wealth is highly concentrated in the form of investment by one person.

Astute capitalists understand that the wealthiest people have extremely high levels of leverage and life options economically, legally, and politically. Frankly, this elite population in many cases has the real ability to "fix the game" in their favor. Constraints levied by the American people through its government to reign in the power and influence of this tiny population is not really as much anti-capitalist, as it is a sane and rational response to strive for an appropriate and sustainable national economic balance and wealth distribution. America must take steps to reverse the gross wealth disparity in the country and to restore the strength and stability of its shrinking middle class.

Aligned with this objective, the American people and its government must not shy from protecting American democracy. These threats are not from foreign invaders, but from the many more numerous and dangerous internal threats to American life. For example, the American government needs to revalidate the founding principles regarding the power of the press and its importance to democracy. The country must recommit to those principles by aggressively reversing the intense consolidation that has occurred in the American media industry over recent decades (for specific details of this important trend, see Consolidation and Control of Media Resources section).

Perhaps of paramount importance is that America's political leadership needs to mandate and somehow provide for a tangibly strong presence of the people's voice during the lawmaking and detailed regulatory process. The voice of the common American citizen must be as competitive, if not stronger, than the voice of big business in setting national policy. Clearly, this is not the state of affairs in America today (this is discussed in detail in the Money and Democracy section).

Also, as part of this effort the government must work toward disentangling the dangerously close associations between itself, the military arm of government, and the dominant private industry interests that stand to profit from American wartime activities. It must be openly acknowledged by political leaders that this association has in fact resulted in the uncomfortable "dangerous triad" which President Eisenhower foresaw. American political leaders must put in place strong remedies and protective measures to extract America out of the business of war.

The executive branch and the military marketing and public relations activities and apparatus should be reevaluated in an open forum by elected public officials, so that American citizens can have a say as to how much of their national taxpayer wealth can be appropriately used to build and sell a case to embark on war.

The option of war must be viewed as an absolutely last resort, and America must not shrink from instituting the strongest of measures to ensure that a march to war is truly the only option. It is not an exaggeration to suggest that a war today opens a path to mass annihilation and global wounds that may be irreparable. A cavalier march to war is immoral; a march to war for profits is criminal.

Executive meetings that are of such broad national import must have an increased level of disclosure to ensure that the American people understand how critical areas of national policy are being formulated, and to provide an ability to verify that the people's interests are being represented. This area of reform suggests changes to information disclosure requirements applying to groups such as the Competitiveness Council, the Defense Policy Board, and the Energy Policy Board. It is clearly dangerous for these meetings to be devoid of voices and interests outside of private industry.

The Senate, the House, and the Judicial Branch must not abdicate its responsibility and duty to balance the power of the Executive Branch, as it has done much too frequently in the past with respect to war and national security concerns. America's founders intentionally separated, organized, and duly empowered the various branches of government for good reason.

Finally, there has been recent temptation in America to move toward intermingling the church and state. The understandable underlying concern is that American government must have a moral underpinning imbued into its policy and actions.

Although many long-term successful civilizations have successfully integrated religion deeply into their government, one example being the Islamic civilization in early world history and today, America is much too diverse in its people to allow government to favor one particular religion over others with respect to its governance. This concept is as American as apple pie. Massive numbers of early American immigrants traveled from Europe specifically to escape from religious persecution and repression.

However, this is not to suggest that moral truths and moral justice can have no part in American domestic and national policy. Or, that because it is secular, America is freed of its moral obligations with respect to its policies. It is rather to suggest that broader humanitarian moral precepts are more appropriate for integration into American government, than specific partisan moral precepts. And most certainly, America should never justify its killing and destruction of humanity in the name of God.

Americans might also want to consider that it would be better in the long run to move away from its reliance on large global corporate entities, and encourage more local and smaller-scale community and commerce. This shift would strengthen the sense of community and promote local sustainable economies and jobs.

Concurrently, the United States government could restructure its corporate tax policies, subsidies, and investments to encourage its large multinational corporations to value people (social value) and natural resources (such as the environment), as highly as it does financial measures (such as profitability). And, to foster new commercial entities that deliver a high level of social and environmental value, as well as financial returns.

Certainly in this restructuring, the entire concept relating to corporate claims to fundamental rights, which were originally intended for people rather than corporate entities, must be reexamined (for a detailed discussion, see Corporate Personhood section). America must be reminded that the original intent by America's founders was that the people would control the country through its government. That the people through their government would grant business interests the privilege to earn profits within that society, provided that they meet constraints and requirements prescribed by the people. Constraints and requirements on private sector activity is a valid precept because the fact is that total freedom of action among market participants usually leads to inequality and not equality.

A Parting Message

At the beginning of this book brief mention was made that referred to the "enlightenment thinkers" who, prior to the American Revolution, planted the seeds of fundamental democratic thought that early American colonists would seize upon to draft their Declaration of Independence from Britain and to construct their own national Constitution.

These enlightenment thinkers asserted various "radical" beliefs. Beliefs that, when taken in aggregate, established a new belief system through which common people could assert their rights and capability for self-governance. This was a radical notion at the time that postulated that the governance of man did not require the rule of a dictator or tyrant.

Inherent in the writings of these enlightenment thinkers was an implied notion of a "united humanity". The belief that there are elements to the human spirit and human conduct that transcend race and national boundaries. The belief that human beings have a good side, and that if a government could be constructed to tap into this good side then common people could effectively, responsibly, and prosperously self-rule.

America is again at a point in history where these beliefs are being tested. The current global war environment is certainly not unique in annuls of human history. Time and time again nations have believed that its national security was under siege, civil liberties have been denied, and military action and invasion has been justified in the name of national security. This is not new.

What is new is that given the accumulated capability of modern weapons technologies, a misstep in direction can credibly signal an end to humanity's brief existence on this planet. Therefore, each step must be carefully considered and must include a genuine sensitivity to the needs of all humans who inhabit earth, and not to the provincial needs and desires of an individual nation.

During times such as these, nations tend to move in one of two different directions. Nations tend to move toward openness and opportunity, or tight control and repression. It can be argued that in the years leading up to and during World War II, America and Germany moved in the two different directions.

During the global economic depression of the early 1900s (somewhat like the world is experiencing today), the fascist regime of Hitler's Nazi party came to power and embarked on an aggressive invasion agenda ostensibly because Germany's homeland security was threatened, and because the Nazis ardently believed that it had a right to claim foreign territories and resources through invasion and aggressive military action. These beliefs were coupled with a strong sense of patriotism, and strong moral judgments and religious beliefs.

Under President Franklin Roosevelt, arguably the most popular President in American history, America embarked on a "New Deal" direction which invested heavily in America's infrastructure, health, education, housing, and the creation of economic growth and jobs for its people. And through the difficult times of the Great Depression and of world war, America emerged stronger.

Hopefully, America is good enough and strong enough today to choose the latter path again, rather than the former path.

If America chooses to invest in its own people, if America chooses positive priorities and directions, and if America can learn to become a productive member of the world community, then the outlook is good for both America and global community. If America chooses a direction fostering repression and global military control, then the outlook is much worse.

American action oriented toward the global good will eventually return to America in the form of domestic good. And conversely, American action oriented toward the global bad will eventually return to America in the form of domestic bad. American must reject greed as a core underlying national value. America must choose to strive to be the Land of the Free, and the Home of the Brave. And reject becoming the Land of the Selfish, and the Home of the Greedy (see statistics in the On Capitalism and Global Resources chapter).

The ideas put forth in this section cannot be narrowly categorized as Democrat ideology or Republican ideology. They are ideology based largely on America's founding principles.

Consider the following questions. If a space alien attacked the earth, would not all nations unite in common defense? Does the world require an attack by a space alien to take the actions required to unite in common defense of the planet? And if so, as one of the world's undisputed economic and military leaders, does America not have a vital responsibility to set an example and tone for this type of united global vision?

If America is made capable to live true to its founding principles, then America will serve as a natural credible example to the people of other nations to consider for their own situation. If people in other countries decide for themselves that a government based on the democratic doctrine is right for their own nation, they can then work internally (as America has done for itself) to make democracy a reality for their own people, and do it in their own way. America should not, and cannot in the long term, force or coerce other nations to adopt its values, principles, and doctrines. This is antithesis to the concept of real freedom. At times, the greatest show of national strength is to *not do* what the country has the power to do.

In an even more enlightened scenario, Americans will be open enough to entertain the notion that Americans do not have all the answers. That Americans can also learn from the people of other countries. That Americans can seek to genuinely understand other values, practices and thought so that they can improve their own governance, culture, and long term sustainability.

Nearing his death, Thomas Jefferson wrote of his hopefulness regarding American's experiment in democracy:

> I will not believe our labors are lost. I shall not die without a hope that light and liberty are on steady advance. And even should the cloud of barbarism and despotism again obscure the science and liberties of Europe. This country remains to preserve and restore light and liberty to them. In short, the flames kindled on the Fourth of July 1776 has spread over too much of the globe to be extinguished by the feeble engines of despotism.

A prominent historian once observed that the American government *is not* America the country. He argued that Americans must learn to distinguish between America (the country and its people) and its anointed government. All governments, including America's, have powers that can be misused. All governments have the capability to lie to and deceive its citizens. Furthermore, governments themselves can even be unpatriotic. America's government was *never* intended by the founders to be "America the country".

In a real democracy, the people establish and grant power to the government in order to serve the wishes of the people. And if the government ever acts against the will of the people, the people have the right and obligation to disband the government and reestablish a new one. This line of thinking was considered foundational to beliefs held dearly by early "enlightenment thinkers", and manifested themselves into American democratic thought. American citizens have great freedoms and choices living under their democratic government. Thus, they also have great innate responsibility whether they want it or not.

A common adage is, "America – Love it or Leave it". If you Love it, perhaps you might be compelled to Stay and Fix it. Perhaps even allow yourself to think and act in the same manner befitting of the early American colonists at the Boston Tea Party. The magic of America has always been that its citizens were compelled to honor their allegiance not to a person, not to a business, and really not even to a government, but rather to an incorruptible set of guiding American principles and ideals.

One thing is certain. The fix will originate from the masses of common people, and certainly not from the government or big business. This has always been true, and will continue to remain true.

List of References

On Human Rights, Civil Rights, Democracy, Liberty, and Freedom

<u>African American Slavery</u>

The Civil War, Geoffrey C. Ward et. al., Alfred A. Knopf, Inc., 1990

A People's History of the United States, Howard Zinn, HarperCollins Publishers, 2003

My Folks Don't Want Me to Talk About Slavery, first hand accounts compiled by Belinda Hurmence, John F. Blair Publisher, 1988

Two Nations: Black and White, Separate, Hostile, Unequal, Andrew Hacker, First Ballantine Books, 1992

The American Experience: John Brown's Holy War, WGBH Educational Foundation, 2000, Video documentary

"Bush Says Slavery One of History's Greatest Crimes", Reuters News Report, 7-8-03

<u>Jim Crow Era</u>

Eyes on the Prize: America at the Racial Crossroads, Blackside Production, Video documentary series

The Civil War, Ken Burns, Video documentary Series

The Rise and Fall of Jim Crow, Quest Productions, VideoLine Productions and Educational Broadcasting Corporation, 2002, Video documentary series

The Strange Demise of Jim Crow, Institute for Medical Humanities, 1997,Video documentary

<u>Ku Klux Klan and Neo Nazism</u>

Frontline: Who is David Duke?, WGBH Educational Foundation, 1992, Video

World Almanac and Book of Facts 2002, World Almanac Education Group, Inc., 2002

Southern Poverty Law Center, Montgomery, Alabama website, www.splcenter.org

The Strange Demise of Jim Crow, Institute for Medical Humanities, 1997,Video documentary

<u>Labor Movement</u>

People's Century: Ordinary People, Extraordinary Times, WGBH Boston Video, 1998, Video documentary

The Fight in the Fields: Cesar Chavez and the Farm Workers' Struggle, Paradigm Productions Inc., Independent Television Service, 1996, Video documentary

Notes on the State of America

Free Market Fantasies: Capitalism in the Real World, Speech by Noam
    Chomsky at Harvard University, recorded by David Barsamian,
    AK Press

Woman's Suffrage Movement
*Not for Ourselves Alone: The Story of Elizabeth Cady Stanton and
    Susan B. Anthony*, Ken Burns, The American Lives Film Project,
    Florentine Films, 1999, Video documentary
*Unequal Protection: The Rise of Corporate Dominance and the Theft of
    Human Rights*, Thom Hartmann, Rodale Inc., 2002

Chinese Exclusion Act and Anti-Chinese Laws
An Illustrated History of Chinese in America, Ruthanne Lum McCunn,
    Design Enterprises of San Francisco, 1979
Bitter Melon: Inside America's Last Rural Chinese Town, Jeff
    Gillenkirk and James Motlow, Heyday Books, 1997
Bridging the Pacific: San Francisco Chinatown and Its People, Thomas
    W. Chinn, Chinese Historical Society of America, 1989
Chinese Women of America, Judy Yung, University of Washington
    Press, 1986

Internment of Japanese, Germans, and Italians
Rabbit in the Moon, Emiko Omori, 1999, Video documentary
A People's History of the United States, Howard Zinn, HarperCollins
    Publishers, 2003
You Back the Attack, We'll Bomb Who We Want, Micah Ian Wright,
    Seven Stories Press, 2003
"Luggage from Home to Camp", essay, San Francisco Chronicle, 8-16-
    03, page D1
*Japanese Latin Americans & the Hostage Exchange Program during
    World War II*, Japanese Peruvian Oral History Project
Japanese Peruvians Present Case for Redress at OAS, Mark Nishimura,
    Hokubei Mainichi newspaper, 7-10-03
*Deportation and Internment of Germans, Japanese, and Italians from
    Latin America during World War II*, Max Friedman, Department
    of History, University of Colorado at Boulder, April 2001

Japan
What Uncle Sam Really Wants, Noam Chomsky, Odonian Press, 1992
Multinational Business Finance, Eighth Edition, David K. Eiteman et.
    al., Addison-Wesley Publishing Company, 1998

Civil Rights Movement
Eyes on the Prize: America at the Racial Crossroads, Blackside
    Production, PBS Video documentary series

List of References

World Almanac and Book of Facts 2002, World Almanac Education
Group, Inc., 2002

Great American Speeches: 80 Years of Political Oratory, Pieri &
Spring Productions, 2000, Video documentary series

Southern Poverty Law Center, Montgomery, Alabama website,
www.splcenter.org

The American Experience: Malcolm X - Make it Plain, Blackside Inc.,
Roja Productions, Video documentary

Joseph McCarthy House Un-American Hearings

"Could It Happen Again?", editorial, San Francisco Chronicle 5-12-03,
page B7

Third World Nationalism

World Almanac and Book of Facts 2002, World Almanac Education
Group, Inc., 2002

What Uncle Sam Really Wants, Noam Chomsky, Odonian Press, 1992

The Roman Empire in the First Century, Goldfarb and Koval
Productions, 2001, Video documentary series

A People's History of the United States, Howard Zinn, HarperCollins
Publishers, 2003

Iran

*All the Shaw's Men: An American Coup and the Roots of Middle East
Terror*, Stephen Kinzer, John Wiley & Sons, 2003

A People's History of the United States, Howard Zinn, HarperCollins
Publishers, 2003

Frontline: Terror and Tehran , 2002, Video documentary

"Iran Nuclear Compliance Questioned", San Francisco Chronicle 6-17-
03, page A10

Haiti

A People's History of the United States, Howard Zinn, HarperCollins
Publishers, 2003

Secrets, Lies and Democracy, Noam Chomsky interviewed by David
Barsamian, Odonian Press, 1994

Brazil

What Uncle Sam Really Wants, Noam Chomsky, Odonian Press, 1992

Fat Cats and Running Dogs: The Enron Stage of Capitalism, Vijay
Prashad, Common Courage Press, 2003

Chile

What Uncle Sam Really Wants, Noam Chomsky, Odonian Press, 1992

Lies My Teacher Told Me, James W. Loewen, Touchstone, 1995

Notes on the State of America

A People's History of the United States, Howard Zinn, HarperCollins
Publishers, 2003

Secrets, Lies and Democracy, Noam Chomsky interviewed by David
Barsamian, Odonian Press, 1994

Gay and Lesbian Movement

Frontline: Assault on Gay America, WGBH Educational Foundation,
2001, Video documentary

The Castro, KQED Inc., 1997

Common Threads: Stories from the Quilt, Telling Pictures Inc. and The
NAMES Project Foundation, 1989

Post-9/11 Foreign Nationals Roundup

"U.S. Report Denounces Round-up After 9/11", San Francisco
Chronicle 6-3-03, page A1

"Interview Would Harm U.S., Court Told", San Francisco Chronicle 6-
4-03, page A3

"Immigrant Jailings Were Mishandled", editorial, San Francisco
Chronicle 6-5-03, page A22

"Patriot Act Too Limited, Ashcroft Says", San Francisco Chronicle 6-6-
03, page A7

"Registered Immigrants Face Deportation", San Francisco Chronicle 6-
7-03, page A1

Center for Constitutional Rights website, www.ccr-ny.org

"Immigration Policies Called Ineffective", San Francisco Chronicle 6-
27-03, page A5

"Justice Department Accused of Rights Abuses", San Francisco
Chronicle 7-21-03, page A3

Guantanamo Bay and Iraq Prisons

*Amnesty International calls on the USA to end legal limbo of
Guantanamo prisoners*, Amnesty International, AMR
51/009/2002, January 2002

"U.S. to Free Several Prisoners in Cuba", San Francisco Chronicle 5-6-
03, page A4

"Time to Unlock American Values", editorial, San Francisco Chronicle
5-6-03, page A18

"Bush Appoints New Overseer to Run Iraq", San Francisco Chronicle 5-
7-03, page A3

"Iraqi Detainees Report 'Inhumane' Handling", San Francisco Chronicle
7-29-03, page A8

"Pentagon Reports New Guantanemo Suicide Attempts", Reuters News
Report, 5-28-03

"Harsh Life for Guantanamo Detainees", San Francisco Chronicle 6-17-
03, page A11

List of References

United Nations (UN) and the Security Council
United Nations website, www.un.org
"The U.N.'s Flag-Waving Fan", San Francisco Chronicle 5-26-03, page
    A2
War on Iraq, Noam Chomsky at the Agape Center in Culver City, CA,
    4-6-03, Video

International Legal Courts
"Blair May Stand Before Court He Championed", editorial, San
    Francisco Chronicle 6-4-03, page A25
"Curbing Lawsuits by Foreign Citizens", San Francisco Chronicle 5-30-
    03, page A19
"Rumsfeld Threatens NATO HQ Over Belgian Crimes Law", Reuters
    News Report, 6-12-03
"U.S. Gets War Crimes Tribunal Exemption", Reuters News Report, 6-
    12-03
"NATO to Regroup Under U.S. Plan to Speed Troops to Global
    Conflicts", San Francisco Chronicle 6-13-03, page A15
"Unocal Seeks Dismissal of Burma Suit", San Francisco Chronicle 6-18-
    03, page A6
"Belgium to Alter War-Crimes Law", San Francisco Chronicle 6-23-03,
    page A8
"U.S. to Halt Aid to 35 Nations", San Francisco Chronicle 7-2-03, page
    A9

Treatment of Military Personnel
"How Will We Welcome Home Those Who Have 'Borne the Battle'",
    editorial, San Francisco Chronicle, 5-26-03, page A17
Direct Orders, Scott Miller, Video documentary
Swords to Plowshares website, www.swords-to-plowshares.org,
"The Forgotten Veterans", editorial, San Francisco Chronicle 5-26-03,
    page A17
You Back the Attack, We'll Bomb Who We Want, Micah Ian Wright,
    Seven Stories Press, 2003

Money and Democracy
Frontline: The Betrayal of Democracy, William Greider, WGBH
    Educational Foundation, 1992, Video documentary
*Unequal Protection: The Rise of Corporate Dominance and the Theft of
    Human Rights*, Thom Hartmann, Rodale Inc., 2002
"Financial Industry Tries and End-Run on Privacy Laws", San Francisco
    Chronicle 8-1-03, page A5
Corporateering: How Corporate Power Steals your Personal Freedom,
    Jamie Court, Jeremy P. Tarcher / Putnam, 2003
Fat Cats and Running Dogs: The Enron Stage of Capitalism, Vijay
    Prashad, Common Courage Press, 2003

Notes on the State of America

"Bush Raising Wads of Money", San Francisco Chronicle 6-22-03, page A1

Frontline: Blackout, WBGH Educational Foundation and The New York Times, 2001, Video documentary

"Uninsured Cost U.S. Up to $130 Billion a Year", Reuters News Report, 6-17-03

Movement toward a Police State

"Fighting for Uncle Sam", editorial, San Francisco Chronicle 6-22-03, page D1

Government by the People – Bill of Rights Edition, Burns et. al., Prentice Hall, 1990

"America's Secret Court: The Foreign Intelligence Surveillance Court", Patrick S. Poole, Free Congress Research and Education Foundation

"Dreaming Behind Bars", editorial, San Francisco Chronicle 6-22-03, page D1

"Citizen in a Strange Land", editorial, San Francisco Chronicle 6-22-03, page D1

You Back the Attack, We'll Bomb Who We Want, Micah Ian Wright, Seven Stories Press, 2003

"Ashcroft Wants Broader Anti-Terror Powers", Associated Press News Report, 6-5-03

"Ashcroft Faces Critics on Patriot Act", Associated Press News Report, 6-5-03

On Weapons and Weapons-of-Mass-Destruction (WMD)

United States Military Spending

Fiscal 2004 Budget of the U. S. Government, U.S. Government Printing Office

"Military Waste Under Fire", San Francisco Chronicle 5-18-03, Page A1

Frontline: Missile Wars, WGBH Educational Foundation, 2002, Video documentary

United States as a Global Weapons Dealer

World Military Expenditures and Arms Transfers 1999-2000, U.S. Department of State, Bureau of Verification and Compliance

"Shaky Cease-Fire in Congo's War", San Francisco Chronicle 5-18-03, page A10

"France to Run Peacekeeping in Bloody Congo – For a While", San Francisco Chronicle 5-29-03, page A10

List of References

"U.N. Peacekeepers Dispatched to Congo", San Francisco Chronicle 5-31-03, page A3

"Specter of Rwanda Looms Over Slaughter in Congo", San Francisco Chronicle 6-1-03, page A18

All Africa website, www.allafrica.com

Global Nuclear Weapons Inventory

SIPRI Yearbook 2002: Armaments, Disarmament and International Security, Stockholm International Peace Research Institute, Oxford University Press

"Bush's Nuclear Arms Plan", San Francisco Chronicle 5-11-03, page A1

Frontline: Kim's Nuclear Gamble, WGBH Educational Foundation, 2003, Video documentary

Frontline: Missile Wars, WGBH Educational Foundation, 2002, Video documentary

Nuclear Weapons Research and Production

"Bush's Nuclear Arms Plan", San Francisco Chronicle 5-11-03, page A1

"Why Congress Butted Heads on Nuke Finding", San Francisco Chronicle 5-25-03, page A1

"U.S. May Build More Warhead Triggers", San Francisco Chronicle 6-3-03, page A10

Chemical Weapons Technology Activity

World Almanac and Book of Facts 2002, World Almanac Education Group, Inc., 2002

SIPRI Yearbook 2002: Armaments, Disarmament and International Security, Stockholm International Peace Research Institute, Oxford University Press

"Army to Destroy Deadly Nerve Agent", San Francisco Chronicle 8-1-03, page A3

"Chemical Weapons Incinerator Fired Up in Alabama", San Francisco Chronicle 8-10-03, page A4

Biological Weapons Technology Activity

World Almanac and Book of Facts 2002, World Almanac Education Group, Inc., 2002

SIPRI Yearbook 2002: Armaments, Disarmament and International Security, Stockholm International Peace Research Institute, Oxford University Press

"Fuss Over Army Plan for Gas Grenade", San Francisco Chronicle 6-9-03, page E1

Hiroshima and Nagasaki

A People's History of the United States, Howard Zinn, HarperCollins Publishers, 2003

Notes on the State of America

War Victims, Howard Zinn at the University of San Diego, 4-3-03
Truman, The American Experience, 1997, Video documentary
"Restored Enola Gay Avoids Controversy", San Francisco Chronicle 8-
    19-03, page A5

Vietnam
You Back the Attack, We'll Bomb Who We Want, Micah Ian Wright,
    Seven Stories Press, 2003

Depleted Uranium
Nuclear Policy Research Institute website, www.nuclearpolicy.org
Democracy Now radio interviews speaking with depleted uranium
    experts.

Cluster Bombs
Frontline: Bombies, Lumiere Productions Inc., 2001, Video
    documentary
"U.S. Under Fire For Use of Cluster Bombs in Iraq", San Francisco
    Chronicle 5-15-03, page A6
"U.S. Gets War Crimes Tribunal Exemption", Reuters News Report, 6-
    12-03
"NATO to Regroup Under U.S. Plan to Speed Troops to Global
    Conflicts", San Francisco Chronicle 6-13-03, page A15

Saddam Hussein's Weapons Supplier
"Who Armed Iraq?", editorial, San Francisco Chronicle 3-2-03, page D1
"Iraqi Council Moves to Create War Crimes Court", San Francisco
    Chronicle 7-16-03, page A10

Military Research Grants
"Blazing the Trail for Tech", San Francisco Chronicle 5-26-03, page B1
Democracy Now radio interview speaking with technology experts
"Pentagon's Futures Market Plan Condemned", Associated Press News
    Report, 7-28-03
"Poindexter to Quit Defense Agency", San Francisco Chronicle 8-1-03,
    page A3

On Terrorism, Torture, Genocide, and Ethnic Cleansing

American Indians
World Almanac and Book of Facts 2002, World Almanac Education
    Group, Inc., 2002
Manufacturing Consent: Noam Chomsky and the Media, Necessary
    Illusions and The National Film Board of Canada, Video
Lies My Teacher Told Me, James W. Loewen, Touchstone, 1995

List of References

What Uncle Sam Really Wants, Noam Chomsky, Odonian Press, 1992
A People's History of the United States, Howard Zinn, HarperCollins
    Publishers, 2003
The Prosperous Few and the Restless Many, Noam Chomsky, Odonian
    Press, 1994

Lynching of African Americans
Eyes on the Prize: America at the Racial Crossroads, Blackside
    Production, Video documentary series
The Civil War, Ken Burns, Video documentary Series

Tuskegee experiment
The Tuskegee Experiment, Video documentary
Bad Blood: The Tuskegee Syphilis Experiment, James H. Jones, Free
    Press, 1993
Remembering Tuskegee, National Public Radio, www.npr.org

Treatment of Conscientious Objectors
The Good War and Those Who Refused to Fight It, Judith Ehrlich and
    Rick Tejada-Flores, Paradigm Productions, Inc., Video
    documentary

South Korea
What Uncle Sam Really Wants, Noam Chomsky, Odonian Press, 1992
Secrets, Lies and Democracy, Noam Chomsky interviewed by David
    Barsamian, Odonian Press, 1994

Guatemala
"Guatemalan Colonel Freed in Notorious Slaying", San Francisco
    Chronicle 5-8-03, page A14
What Uncle Sam Really Wants, Noam Chomsky, Odonian Press, 1992
A People's History of the United States, Howard Zinn, HarperCollins
    Publishers, 2003
Discovering Dominga, Patricia Flynn, Jaguar House Film, 2002, Video
    documentary

El Salvador
What Uncle Sam Really Wants, Noam Chomsky, Odonian Press, 1992
A People's History of the United States, Howard Zinn, HarperCollins
    Publishers, 2003

East Timor
Manufacturing Consent: Noam Chomsky and the Media, Necessary
    Illusions and The National Film Board of Canada, Video
Wages of War, British Pathe, Trans World International, 1998, Video
    documentary

Notes on the State of America

What Uncle Sam Really Wants, Noam Chomsky, Odonian Press, 1992
"Wolfowitz Criticizes Indonesian Military", San Francisco Chronicle 5-31-03, page A12

Vietnam, Cambodia, and Laos
Vietnam, The American Experience, Video documentary
Manufacturing Consent: Noam Chomsky and the Media, Necessary
    Illusions and The National Film Board of Canada, Video
A People's History of the United States, Howard Zinn, HarperCollins
    Publishers, 2003
What Uncle Sam Really Wants, Noam Chomsky, Odonian Press, 1992
Fat Cats and Running Dogs: The Enron Stage of Capitalism, Vijay
    Prashad, Common Courage Press, 2003
Government by the People – Bill of Rights Edition, Burns et. al., Prentice
    Hall, 1990

Afghanistan
You Back the Attack, We'll Bomb Who We Want, Micah Ian Wright,
    Seven Stories Press, 2003
"Stress and Duress' Tactics Used on Terrorism Suspects Held in Secret
    Overseas Facilities", Washington Post, 12-26-02
"Film Exposing Pentagon War Crimes Premieres in U.S.", Bill Vann, 2-12-2003
Afghan Massacre: The Convoy of Death, Atlantic Celtic Films, Jamie
    Doran, 2003, Video documentary
"Award-winning Director and Producer Jamie Doran Alleges a Media
    Cover-Up of US Complicity in the Massacre of up to 2,000
    Taliban Prisoners", Democracy Now, 5-26-03

Western Hemisphere Institute for Security Cooperation (WHINSEC)
A People's History of the United States, Howard Zinn, HarperCollins
    Publishers, 2003
Hidden in Plain Sight, Ravens Call Productions, Video documentary
"School of Americas Protest", Sharon Abercrombie, USF in the News,
    Summer 2003

On Capitalism and Global Resources

Wealth Distribution in America and the World
Dominance and the Theft of Human Rights, Thom Hartmann, Rodale
    Inc., 2002
Free Market Fantasies: Capitalism in the Real World, Speech by Noam
    Chomsky at Harvard University, recorded by David Barsamian,
    AK Press

List of References

Global Environment Outlook 3, United Nations Environment
    Programme, Earthscan Publications Ltd., 2002

"Cadence says Jobs to Move Overseas", San Francisco Chronicle 8-25-
    03, page E1

The Peace of Health, Teresa Walsh, USF Magazine of the University of
    San Francisco, 2003

"Thanks for Nothing", editorial, San Francisco Chronicle 5-28-03, page
    B1

Very Richest's Share of Wealth Grew Even Bigger Data Show, New
    York Times, 6-26-03, A1

"Record Federal Deficit Forecast", San Francisco Chronicle 7-16-03,
    page A1

"The U.S. Ignores a Region in Crisis", San Francisco Chronicle 7-27-03,
    page D1

Dividend Voodoo, Warren Buffet, Washington Post, 5-20-03, page A19

"Troops in Iraq Face Pay Cut", San Francisco Chronicle 8-14-03, page
    A1

Consumption in America and the World

Macmillan Encyclopedia of Energy, John Zumerchik, Macmillan
    Reference USA, 2001

World Almanac and Book of Facts 2002, World Almanac Education
    Group, Inc., 2002

Secrets, Lies and Democracy, Noam Chomsky interviewed by David
    Barsamian, Odonian Press, 1994

Pollution and Waste in America and the World

Macmillan Encyclopedia of Energy, John Zumerchik, Macmillan
    Reference USA, 2001

World Almanac and Book of Facts 2002, World Almanac Education
    Group, Inc., 2002

Global Environment Outlook 3, United Nations Environment
    Programme, Earthscan Publications Ltd., 2002

"Don't Cry for Christie", editorial, San Francisco Chronicle 5-22-03,
    page A25

Federal Tax Revenues

*Unequal Protection: The Rise of Corporate Dominance and the Theft of
    Human Rights*, Thom Hartmann, Rodale Inc., 2002

Statistical Abstract of the United States 2002, U. S. Department of
    Commerce, Economics and Statistics Administration, U. S. Census
    Bureau

Corporateering: How Corporate Power Steals your Personal Freedom,
    Jamie Court, Jeremy P. Tarcher / Putnam, 2003

Notes on the State of America

Oil Interests

US Energy Security Facts, Rocky Mountain Institute website,
www.rmi.org

The Party's Over: Oil, War and the Fate of Industrial Societies,
Richard Heinberg, New Society Publishers, 2003

World Almanac and Book of Facts 2002, World Almanac Education
Group, Inc., 2002

Macmillan Encyclopedia of Energy, John Zumerchik, Macmillan
Reference USA, 2001

San Francisco Chronicle 5-12-03, page I2

Why Economies Grow, Jeff Madrick, Century Foundation, 2002

America's Crisis of Confidence

Frontline: The Wallstreet Fix, WGBH Educational Foundation, 2003,
Video documentary

Frontline: Dotcon, WGBH Educational Foundation, 2002, Video
documentary

The Deal, page 25, 6-2-03

"U.S. Halts Business with WorldCom", San Francisco Chronicle 8-1-03,
page B1

*Unequal Protection: The Rise of Corporate Dominance and the Theft of
Human Rights*, Thom Hartmann, Rodale Inc., 2002

Fat Cats and Running Dogs: The Enron Stage of Capitalism, Vijay
Prashad, Common Courage Press, 2003

"Big Names in Corporate Fraud Go Free", San Francisco Chronicle, 8-
14-03, page B1

"Judge, SEC Set Modest MCI Fine", San Francisco Chronicle 7-8-03,
page B1

Enron's Bankers: A Great Prison Escape, Emily Thornton and Mike
France, Businessweek Commentary, 7-31-03

60 Minutes: Montana Power, James Kraft, 8-10-03 Video

Corporate Personhood

*Unequal Protection: The Rise of Corporate Dominance and the Theft of
Human Rights*, Thom Hartmann, Rodale Inc., 2002

Our Flag, 107th Congress, 1st Session, U.S. Government Printing Office,
Washington, 2001

The Great Declaration, Henry Steele Commager, Eastern Acorn Press,
1982

The Great Constitution, Henry Steele Commager, Eastern Acorn Press,
1982

Store Wars, Teddy Bear Films, 2001

List of References

Corporate Subsidies and Supports

Free Market Fantasies: Capitalism in the Real World, Speech by Noam
  Chomsky at Harvard University, recorded by David Barsamian,
  AK Press
Frontline: The Betrayal of Democracy, William Greider, WGBH
  Educational Foundation, 1992, Video documentary
Secrets, Lies and Democracy, Noam Chomsky interviewed by David
  Barsamian, Odonian Press, 1994
"Broad Cut in Corporate Taxes Proposed", San Francisco Chronicle 7-
  25-03, page B2

The Lost Commons

*Unequal Protection: The Rise of Corporate Dominance and the Theft of
  Human Rights*, Thom Hartmann, Rodale Inc., 2002
"Federal Probe Widens", San Francisco Chronicle 6-3-03, page B1
"White House Removes Some Logging Hurdles", San Francisco
  Chronicle 5-31-03, page A1
Frontline: Blackout, WBGH Educational Foundation and The New
  York Times, 2001, Video documentary
"Enron Power Trader Taken Off to Jail", San Francisco Chronicle 6-4-
  03, page B1
"Debate Rages Over Who Will Run Iraq's Utilities", San Francisco
  Chronicle 6-8-03, page I1
"Bush Orders Speed-Up of Energy Extraction in the West", San
  Francisco Chronicle 8-8-03, page A4
Corporateering: How Corporate Power Steals your Personal Freedom,
  Jamie Court, Jeremy P. Tarcher / Putnam, 2003
"Dying Early Saves Money, Tobacco Company Says", Gordon
  Fairclough, Wall Street Journal, July 12, 2001
60 Minutes: Montana Power, James Kraft, 8-10-03 Video
Corporate Warriors: The Rise of the Privatized Military Industry, by
  P.W. Singer, Cornell University Press, 2003

International Trade

Multinational Business Finance, Eighth Edition, David K. Eiteman et.
  al., Addison-Wesley Publishing Company, 1998
Free Market Fantasies: Capitalism in the Real World, Speech by Noam
  Chomsky at Harvard University, recorded by David Barsamian,
  AK Press
Secrets, Lies and Democracy, Noam Chomsky interviewed by David
  Barsamian, Odonian Press, 1994

Immigrant Labor

An Illustrated History of Chinese in America, Ruthanne Lum McCunn,
  Design Enterprises of San Francisco, 1979

Notes on the State of America

Racial and Ethnic Groups in America, Juan L. Gonzales, Jr., Kendall / Hunt Publishing Company, 1990

Reefer Madness: Sex, Drugs, and Cheap Labor in the American Black Market, Eric Schlosser, Houghton Mifflin Company, 2003

World Trade Organization (WTO)

World Trade Organization website, www.wto.int

"EU Defies U.S. in Row over Genetically Modified Foods", Stefania Bianchi, Inter Press Service, 2003

World Almanac and Book of Facts 2002, World Almanac Education Group, Inc., 2002

International Monetary Fund (IMF) and United Nations World Bank

World Almanac and Book of Facts 2002, World Almanac Education Group, Inc., 2002

Fat Cats and Running Dogs: The Enron Stage of Capitalism, Vijay Prashad, Common Courage Press, 2003

United States Export-Import Bank (Ex-Im) and Overseas Private Investment Corporation (OPIC)

World Almanac and Book of Facts 2002, World Almanac Education Group, Inc., 2002

Fat Cats and Running Dogs: The Enron Stage of Capitalism, Vijay Prashad, Common Courage Press, 2003

Corporateering: How Corporate Power Steals your Personal Freedom, Jamie Court, Jeremy P. Tarcher / Putnam, 2003

Electronic International Financial Transactions

Free Market Fantasies: Capitalism in the Real World, Speech by Noam Chomsky at Harvard University, recorded by David Barsamian, AK Press

On International Aggression

Project for a New American Century website, www.newamericancentury.org

Rebuilding America's Defenses: Strategy, Forces and Resources for a New Century, Project for the New American Century, September 2000

"U.S. Returns to the Path to Destruction", editorial, San Francisco Chronicle 5-14-03, page A19

"The Man Behind 'Total War' in the Mid East", editorial, San Francisco Chronicle 5-14-03, page A19

List of References

Mexico

A People's History of the United States, Howard Zinn, HarperCollins
    Publishers, 2003

Cuba

"Leave Iraq Before U.S. Becomes Too Invested", USA Today, 4-22-03,
    page 13A
What Uncle Sam Really Wants, Noam Chomsky, Odonian Press, 1992

Panama

What Uncle Sam Really Wants, Noam Chomsky, Odonian Press, 1992
The Prosperous Few and the Restless Many, Noam Chomsky, Odonian
    Press, 1994
You Back the Attack, We'll Bomb Who We Want, Micah Ian Wright,
    Seven Stories Press, 2003
A Man, A Plan, A Canal: Panama, David McCullough, WGBH
    Production, Video documentary
A People's History of the United States, Howard Zinn, HarperCollins
    Publishers, 2003

Philippines

Leave Iraq Before U.S. Becomes Too Invested, USA Today, 4-22-03,
    page 13A
A People's History of the United States, Howard Zinn, HarperCollins
    Publishers, 2003
"Fighting for Uncle Sam", San Francisco Chronicle 6-22, page D1

Hawaii

The Rise and Fall of the Hawaiian Kingdom, Richard A. Wisniewski,
    Pacific Basin Enterprises, 1979
Troubled Paradise, Farallon Films Production, Steven Okazaki
NPR Radio, Interviews with ex-Hawaiian plantation workers, 2003

Nicaragua

A People's History of the United States, Howard Zinn, HarperCollins
    Publishers, 2003
What Uncle Sam Really Wants, Noam Chomsky, Odonian Press, 1992
Secrets, Lies and Democracy, Noam Chomsky interviewed by David
    Barsamian, Odonian Press, 1994
 "Albert Hakim – Money Architect of Iran-Contra Deals", obituary, San
    Francisco Chronicle 4-30-03, page A21

Grenada

What Uncle Sam Really Wants, Noam Chomsky, Odonian Press, 1992

Notes on the State of America

Somalia

The Prosperous Few and the Restless Many, Noam Chomsky, Odonian Press, 1994

The Common Good, Noam Chomsky interviewed by David Barsamian, Odonian Press, 1998

A People's History of the United States, Howard Zinn, HarperCollins Publishers, 2003

Sudan

CNN Report, 8-22-98

Open Letter to the Right Honourable Robin Cook MP British Foreign Secretary, The Sudan Foundation, October 1998

9-11, Noam Chomsky, Seven Stories Press, 2001

Israel

Statistical Abstract of the United States 2002, U. S. Department of Commerce, Economics and Statistics Administration, U. S. Census Bureau

"U.S. May Pressure Israel Financially", San Francisco Chronicle 8-5-03, page A3

The Prosperous Few and the Restless Many, Noam Chomsky, Odonian Press, 1994

Frontline: Battle for the Holy Land, WGBH Educational Foundation, 2002, Video documentary

Gaza Strip, James Longley, 2001, Video documentary

"Hamas Committed to Armed Struggle Against Israel", San Francisco Chronicle 6-14-03, page A14

"Pelosi Supports Israel's Attacks on Hamas Group", San Francisco Chronicle 6-14-03, page A14

"Legacy of the Six-Day War", San Francisco Chronicle 6-17-03, page A23

At What Price?, Gershom Gorenberg, Mother Jones Magazine, 2003

Arab and Jew: Wounded Spirits in a Promised Land, David K. Shipler, New York Times book, 1986

"Zionists Find Ally in DeLay", San Francisco Chronicle 7-31-03, page A8

Afghanistan

Charlie Wilson's War: The Extraordinary Story of the Largest Covert Operation in History, George Crile, Atlantic Monthly, 2003.

Biography: Osama Bin Laden: In the name of Allah, ABC News Inc. and A&E Networks, 2001

Bin Laden: The Man Who Declared War on America, Yossef Bodansky, Prima Publishing, 2001

Wages of War, British Pathe, Trans World International, 1998, Video documentary

List of References

Afghanistan: Captives of the Warlords, Fast Forward Films Limited, Detroit Public Television, 2001, Video

Iraq
"Leave Iraq Before U.S. Becomes Too Invested", USA Today, 4-22-03, page 13A

You Back the Attack, We'll Bomb Who We Want, Micah Ian Wright, Seven Stories Press, 2003

"Baghdad Casualties Tallied", San Francisco Chronicle 5-18-03, Page A12

"For Iraq's Children, a New War Has Begun", San Francisco Chronicle 5-18-03, Page A1

What Uncle Sam Really Wants, Noam Chomsky, Odonian Press, 1992

60 Minutes II: Saddam (interview), 2003

Frontline: The War Behind Closed Doors, WGBH Educational Foundation, 2003, Video documentary

"U.S. Returns to the Path to Destruction", editorial, San Francisco Chronicle 5-14-03, page A19

"U.S. Ban Will Strip Guns from Iraqis", San Francisco Chronicle 5-21-03, page A12

Financial Times, 5-26-03

"Iraq War Rationale Questioned Anew", San Francisco Chronicle 5-31-03, page A1

"Activists Must Be in For the Long Haul, Because Change Takes Time", editorial, San Francisco Chronicle 6-1-03, page D1

"U.S. Drops Assembly Idea for Interim Political Council", San Francisco Chronicle 6-2-03, page A3

"Panel to Probe Failure to Find Banned Arms", San Francisco Chronicle 6-2-03, page A3

AFP newswire report, 5-30-03

"Spy Report on Iraq's Weapons Questioned", San Francisco Chronicle 6-4-03, page A15

"Blair Pressured on Iraq Weapons", San Francisco Chronicle 6-4-03, page A15

"Iraq War has Damaged U.S. Image, Poll Finds", San Francisco Chronicle 6-4-03, page A1

"Ex-Official: Evidence Distorted for War", Associated Press News Report, 6-7-03

"AP Tallies 3,240 Civilian Deaths in Iraq", Associate Press News Report, 6-10-03

Iraq Fatality Count Website, www.iraqbodycount.net

"War Claimed 3,240 Civilians", San Francisco Chronicle 6-11-03, page A3

Public Radio interview with Senator Carl Levin 6-17-03

"Troops in Iraq Face Pay Cut", San Francisco Chronicle 8-14-03, page A1

"Politics Challenged Analysis of Iraq, Official Tells Panels", San
Francisco Chronicle 6-25-03, page A18

"White House Says Iraq Uranium Claim Forged", Reuters News Report,
7-8-03

"Imports Inundate Iraq Under New U.S. Policy", San Francisco
Chronicle 7-10-03, page A1

"Iraqi Oil Would be Collateral for Loans Under Bank's Plan", San
Francisco Chronicle 7-11-03, page A10

"Ex-Officials Dispute Iraq Tie to al-Qaida", Associated Press News
Report, 7-13-03

"Tab on Iraq War Could Limit Other Military Funding", San Francisco
Chronicle 7-13-03, page A12

"Iraq Pieces Together Its First Postwar Governing Council", San
Francisco Chronicle 7-13-03, page A12

"Bush Doublespeak", editorial, San Francisco Chronicle 7-14-03, page
B7

"Prewar Intelligence Failures Merit Investigation", San Francisco
Chronicle 7-15-03, page A21

"Iraq Link to Terror Judged Not Likely Before Bush Speech", San
Francisco Chronicle 7-21-03, page A5

"Allies Rewarded with Trade Pacts", San Francisco Chronicle 5-11-03,
page I1

KPFA Pacific News radio report, 7-21-03

"Senators Put the Heat on Wolfowitz", San Francisco Chronicle 7-30-
03, page A15

"Bechtel Given Details on Projects to do in Iraq", San Francisco
Chronicle 7-30-03, page A1

Weapons of Mass Deception, Sheldon Rampton and John Stauber,
Tarcher / Penguin Books, 2003

"Mandela Calls for Condemnation of Bush", San Francisco Chronicle
6-28-03, page A10

"Pentagon Sees Growing Chinese Threat to Taiwan", Reuters News
Report, 7-30-03

"U.S. Official Says North Korea a "Hellish Nightmare"", Reuters News
Report, 7-30-03

"Report says Saudis Aided 9/11 Hijackers", San Francisco Chronicle 8-
2-03, page A1

"Career Officer Does Eye-Opening Stint Inside Pentagon", Karen
Kwiatkowski, Ohio Beacon Journal, 7-31-03

On the Media

Consolidation and Control of Media Resources
Manufacturing Consent: Noam Chomsky and the Media, Necessary
Illusions and The National Film Board of Canada, Video

List of References

"S.F. Picketers Protest Vote on New FCC Rules", San Francisco
 Chronicle 5-30-03, page B1

Democracy Now radio broadcast reports regarding media consolidation

Manufacturing Consent: The Political Economy of the Mass Media,
 Edward S. Herman and Noam Chomsky, Pantheon Books, 1988

Media Techniques

News Reporting and Writing, 4th Edition, Melvin Mencher, Wm. C.
 Brown Publishers, 1984

*Newstalk II: State-of-the-Art Conversations with Today's Broadcast
 Journalists*, Shirley Biagi, Wadsworth Publishing Company, 1987

Headlines and the Buried Real Story

"Bush Off on Tour of 6 Nations", San Francisco Chronicle 5-31-03,
 page A14

"CIA Asked to Explain Reports on Iraqi Arms", San Francisco
 Chronicle 5-31-03, page A14

"Bush Calls on Europe to Help Vanquish Evil", San Francisco Chronicle
 6-1-03, page A1

Manufacturing Consent: Noam Chomsky and the Media, Necessary
 Illusions and The National Film Board of Canada, Video

"U.S. Drops Assembly Idea for Interim Political Council", San
 Francisco Chronicle 6-2-03, page A3

Americans Out of Step With the World

"Bush Has Much to Explain", editorial, San Francisco Chronicle 6-22-
 03, page D4

"The Psychology of Fanaticism", editorial, San Francisco Chronicle 6-
 22-03, page D4

What Uncle Sam Really Wants, Noam Chomsky, Odonian Press, 1992

A Frightened Population

Bowling For Columbine, Michael Moore, MGM, 2002, Video
 documentary movie

Manufacturing Consent: Noam Chomsky and the Media, Necessary
 Illusions and The National Film Board of Canada, Video

From Nuremberg to Nuremberg, Antenne 2 / CDG, Jean Frydman,
 1988, Video documentary series

Media Bias

Manufacturing Consent: Noam Chomsky and the Media, Necessary
 Illusions and The National Film Board of Canada, Video

Notes on the State of America

Big Business

Legislative Issue Advertising in the 107th Congress, Erika Falk, Annenberg Public Policy Center of the University of Pennsylvania, 2003

Unequal Protection: The Rise of Corporate Dominance and the Theft of Human Rights, Thom Hartmann, Rodale Inc., 2002

Government and the Media

Manufacturing Consent: Noam Chomsky and the Media, Necessary Illusions and The National Film Board of Canada, Video

Fighting for the First Amendment: Stanton of CBS versus Congress and the Nixon White House, Corydon B. Dunham, 1997, Praeger Publishers

Weapons of Mass Deception, Sheldon Rampton and John Stauber, Tarcher / Penguin Books, 2003

Military and the Media

Fighting for the First Amendment: Stanton of CBS versus Congress and the Nixon White House, Corydon B. Dunham, 1997, Praeger Publishers

"Iraq War Rationale Questioned Anew", San Francisco Chronicle 5-31-03, page A1

"When Do Our Troops Leave for Congo?", San Francisco Chronicle 6-1-03, page D4

"Panel to Probe Failure to Find Banned Arms", San Francisco Chronicle 6-2-03, page A3

"NBC Tries to Save 'Lynch'", San Francisco Chronicle 6-4-03, page D1

What Uncle Sam Really Wants, Noam Chomsky, Odonian Press, 1992

"Giving Good War", San Francisco Chronicle 6-15-03, page D1

Weapons of Mass Deception: The Uses of Propaganda in Bush's War on Iraq, Sheldon Rampton, John C. Stauber, J. P. Tarcher, 2003

Deregulation of the Media

"Playing Media Monopoly", The Deal, 5-19-03, page 8

"Limits on Media Ownership Eased", San Francisco Chronicle 6-3-03, page A1

Radio speeches and comments by Michael Copps, FCC commissioner

On the Dangerous Triad

War, Money, Corporations and the Government

World Almanac and Book of Facts 2002, World Almanac Education Group, Inc., 2002

Wages of War, British Pathe, Trans World International, 1998, Video documentary

List of References

"Hopeful Firms Line Up to Score Work in Iraq", San Francisco
Chronicle 5-22-03, page B1

"Halliburton's Iraq Contract Bigger Than First Reported", San Francisco
Chronicle, 5-7-03, page A8

"WorldCom Iraq Deal Blasted", San Francisco Chronicle 5-22-03, page
B3

"Army's Iraq Contracts Under Fire", San Francisco Chronicle, 5-30-03,
page B2

"Chemical Weapons Cleanup Shared", San Francisco Chronicle 6-17-
03, page B3

"Judge, SEC Set Modest MCI Fine", San Francisco Chronicle 7-8-03,
page B1

Defense Policy Board
*Advisors of Influence: Nine Members of the Defense Policy Board Have
Ties to Defense Contractors*, Center for Public Integrity, 3-28-03

Diego Garcia
Diego Garcia, 60 Minutes CBS report, Christiane Amanpour, 6-15-03

Other References

Civilizations: Ten Thousand Years of Ancient History, Jane McIntosh &
Clint Twist, DK Publishing, Inc., 2001

The Umbrella of U.S. Power, Noam Chomsky, Seven Stories Press,
1997

*Thomas Jefferson, Ken Burns, The American Lives Film Project,
Florentine Films, 1997, Video* documentar

*Fortunate Son: George W. Bush and the Making of an American
President*, J. H. Hatfield, Omega Publishing Endeavours, Inc.,
2001

Islam: Empire of Faith, narrated by Ben Kingsley, Video documentary

Mark Twain, Ken Burns, The American Lives Film Project, Florentine
Films, 2001, Video documentary

From Nuremberg to Nuremberg, Antenne 2 / CDG, Jean Frydman,
1988, Video documentary series

Fast Food Nation, Eric Schlosser, HarperCollins Publishers, 2002

About the Writer

Craighton E. Gee is a consultant and executive for companies developing renewable energy and other environmentally clean technologies. He holds an engineering degree from the University of California at Berkeley, and an MBA in International Business and Finance from the University of San Francisco.

Mr. Gee has worked for a number of high technology companies, including multinational corporations. His interests include international business and trade, social ventures, finance, technology, and government. Mr. Gee has traveled internationally, and he has served locally on government commissions and as a consultant to public sector agencies. He has also worked with and supported various non-profit and community organizations. Mr. Gee is a third generation San Franciscan, and remains enamored with the Bay Area.

Index

Index

Index

Index

Index

Index